VISIONS AND VISIONARIES

VISIONS & VISIONARIES

THE ART & ARTISTS OF THE SANTA FE RAILWAY

Sandra D'Emilio and Suzan Campbell

PEREGRINE SMITH BOOKS

SALT LAKE CITY

First edition

94 93 92 91   5 4 3 2 1

This is a Peregrine Smith Book, published by
Gibbs Smith, Publisher
P.O. Box 667
Layton, UT 84041

Design by Randall Smith
Manufactured by Times Offset Pte Ltd, Singapore

Cover Illustrations
Front: *Evening at Pueblo at Taos* by Ernest L. Blumenschein
Back: Photo courtesy of The Museum of New Mexico, neg. #47181

ISBN 0-87905-382-8

To our dear families and fabulous friends

FOREWORD

A S one who has spent a large part of the past twenty-four years involved with the Atchison, Topeka and Santa Fe Railway Company's collection of southwestern art, I welcome the efforts of this volume's two authors. By discussing the collection's beginnings and exploring the strong links between the railway and the growth of the artist colonies in New Mexico, Sandra D'Emilio and Suzan Campbell have provided both an accurate and interesting history of the Santa Fe Collection of Southwestern Art.

Accounts of the development and history of the Fred Harvey Company further illuminate the fascinating relationships that existed between businesses and artists in the late nineteenth and early twentieth centuries—a time of great growth and increasing recognition in the United States of the importance of southwestern art. While the bulk of the Santa Fe Collection is housed at the railway's headquarters in Schaumburg, Illinois—where paintings decorate private offices and public hallways—a number of individual pieces reside at railway and subsidiary offices in Los Angeles, Albuquerque, Topeka, and Houston. Additional paintings are held in reserve and are displayed two or three times a year while the exhibit group is on loan. Since the Santa Fe's efforts toward sharing the collection with the public were initiated in 1966, there have been more than sixty exhibits of our paintings in museums and cultural centers throughout the area served by the Santa Fe, as well as at the National Archives in Washington, D.C.

Throughout the existence of the collection, railway management and employees have shown an active appreciation of the art and artists represented. Being involved in the exhibit program has given me a unique perspective on the positive corporate and public value of the art in Santa Fe's collection. It is meant to be shared.

> —Paul Benisek
> Curator
> Santa Fe Collection of Southwestern Art

ACKNOWLEDGEMENT

THANK you to Gibbs Smith, Publisher, Peregrine Smith Books for having the insight to publish this book and to the following staff for all their expertise: Madge Baird, Editor, Steve Chapman, Publicity, and Randall Smith, Design.

So many people were extremely helpful with their assistance for this project. Without them, it would have been impossible to complete all the necessary work involved. In particular, Paul D. Benisek, Curator, The Santa Fe Collection of Southwestern Art, Chicago; Rose and George Kaplan, Research Assistants, Santa Fe; Connie Harper, Research Assistant, Santa Fe; Elizabeth Cunningham, Curator, The Anschutz Collection, Denver; Phyllis Gladden, Research Assistant, Albuquerque; Mark Adams, Gene White, and Jeanette Baca de Lovato, Inter-Library Loan Staff, New Mexico State Library, Santa Fe; and Theresa Arellano, Secretary, Museum of Fine Arts, Museum of New Mexico, Santa Fe, deserve our very special thanks.

The following people and institutions generously provided scholarly and photographic assistance and helpful advice: Robert E. Gehrt, former Vice President, Public Relations, and Catherine Westphal, Manager, Public Affairs, the Atchison, Topeka and Santa Fe Railway Company, Chicago; Connie Menniger, Archivist, and Darrell D. Garwood, Photo Archivist, Kansas State Historical Society, Topeka; Neil Posse, Director, Victor Grant, Archivist, Kit Carson Historic Museums, Taos; Peggy Giltrow, Reference Librarian, New Mexico State Library, Santa Fe; Gene Noss, Librarian, University of New Mexico Fine Arts Library, Albuquerque; Virginia Couse Leavitt, Couse Family Archives, Tucson; Barbara B. Brenner, Taos Heritage Publishing Co., Taos; Dean A. Porter, Director, Snite Museum of Art, Notre Dame, Indiana; Michael Grauer, Curator, and Dorothy Johnson, Assistant Archivist/Librarian, Panhandle-Plains Historical Museum, Canyon, Texas; Alta Ann Morris, New York, Ed Muno, Curator, National Cowboy Hall of Fame and Western Heritage Center, Oklahoma City; Genni Houlihan, Library Assistant, Phoenix Art Museum, Phoenix; Carol Whitney, Chairman, Board of Trustees, The Jacobson Foundation, Norman, Oklahoma; Suzanne Kenagy, Research Assistant, Santa Fe; Walt Wiggins, Wiggins Gallery,

Santa Fe; John W. Smith, Chief Archivist, and Andrew Martinez, Assistant Archivist, Art Institute of Chicago, Chicago; Mario Klimiades, Librarian/Archivist, Kathy Howard, Guild Member, and Jim Reynolds, Native American Artist Files Project Assistant, Heard Museum Library, Phoenix; Carol Burke, Photo. Archivist, Museum of Northern Arizona, Flagstaff; Martha W. Ross, Curator, Saginaw Art Museum, Saginaw, Michigan; Beatrice Chauvenet, Author, Albuquerque; Lesley Poling-Kempes, Author, Abiquiu, New Mexico; Mildred Bruder Buchanan, Taos; Barbara Kittle, Librarian, The University of Arizona, Tucson; Judy Hudson, Curator, Valley National Bank, Phoenix; David Witt, Curator, The Harwood Foundation of the University of New Mexico, Taos; Deborah Flynn, Photo Archivist, School of American Research, Santa Fe; Kraushaar Galleries, New York; Bob and Marianne Kapour, The Rainbow Man, Santa Fe; Robin Oldham, Archivist, Citizens Committee for Historical Preservation, Las Vegas; Barbara Thurber, Library Assistant, Museum of Northern Arizona, Flagstaff; David B. Winton, son-in-law of E. Martin Hennings, Lincolnshire, Illinois; Katherine Sayre, former Executive Secretary to Major R. Hunter Clarkson, Santa Fe; Ann Brown, Archivist, Fenn Galleries, Santa Fe; Richard Salazar, Chief Archivist, Sandy Macias, Archivist, Alfred Aragon, Archivist, Robert Torrez, Archivist, Ron Montoya, Archivist, and Al Regensberg, Archivist, New Mexico State Records Center and Archives, Santa Fe; Robert Kuegel, Registrar, Tucson Museum of Art, Tucson; Sharyn R. Udall, Art Historian, Santa Fe; Robert R. White, Art Historian, Albuquerque; James Arender, Santa Fe; Eliza M. Williams, Executive Secretary, La Fonda, Santa Fe; Barbara Kittle, Librarian, University of Arizona Museum of Art, Tucson; Dorothy Haines, Volunteer, Painting and Sculpture Library, Denver Art Museum, Denver; Joslyn Art Museum, Omaha; Barbara Kramer, Research Assistant, Santa Fe; Joyce Vaughn, Director, Jane Gillespie, Sales Department, El Tovar Hotel, Grand Canyon; Joseph Traugott, Curator, Jonson Gallery, University of New Mexico, Albuquerque; Juanita Dennard and Brian Dennard, Albuquerque; Gretchen Faulkner, Director, Hudson Museum, University of Maine, Orono, Maine; Patricia Steindler, Research Assistant, Santa Fe; Gordon Lindsey, Research Assistant, Santa Fe; the late Alfred "Chan" Hunt, San Francisco; Alfred Johnson, San Francisco; Ruth Greig, Santa Fe; John Meigs, San Patricio, New Mexico; and

James R. Marmon, Bandelier National Monument, for his continuous support; and Gage Holland, for being an understanding friend.

Appreciation also for their insight and personal interviews to the following: Edmund Ladd, Curator of Ethnology, Laboratory of Anthropology, Museum of New Mexico, Santa Fe; Ila McAfee, Artist, Taos; Robert H. Clarkson, son of Major R. Hunter Clarkson, Albuquerque; Richard Hill, Museum Director, Institute of American Indian Arts, Santa Fe; Don Van Soelen, son of Theodore Van Soelen, Santa Fe; and Henry Sauerwein, Director, Helene Wurlitzer Foundation, Taos.

Special gratitude also for their assistance and expertise to the following staff at the Museum of New Mexico, Santa Fe: David Turner, Director, Phyllis Cohen, Librarian, Rusty Andrews, Library Volunteer, Museum of Fine Arts; Bruce Bernstein, Assistant Director/Chief Curator, Museum of Indian Arts and Culture; Orlando Romero, Research Librarian, Palace of the Governors; Richard Rudisill, Curator of Photographic History; Arthur Olivas, Archivist; and Blair Clark, Photographer.

Finally, to our dear families and fabulous friends, this publication is warmly dedicated.

Sandra D'Emilio and Suzan Campbell

INTRODUCTION

". . . I do like having the big, unbroken spaces round me. There is something savage, unbreakable in the spirit of place out here . . ."

—D. H. Lawrence[1]

". . . the future of American art lies in being true to our own country, in the interpretation of that beautiful and glorious scenery with which nature has so lavishly endowed our land . . . My chief desire is to call the attention of American landscape painters to the unlimited field for the exercise of their talents to be found in this enchanting southwestern country; a country flooded with color and picturesqueness, offering everything to inspire the artist. . . ."

—Thomas Moran[2]

The Spirit of Place

In 1892, flamboyant, popular explorer-journalist Charles Fletcher Lummis captured the nation's imagination with descriptions of his walk from Cincinnati to Los Angeles, following, when he could, the route of the Santa Fe Trail. For Lummis, as for those who followed him, discovery of the American West endowed possession: "My name is Lummis, I'm the West!" he exulted,

> For Culture I don't give a hang;
> I hate the puny East, although
> I can't conceal my Yankee twang
> My trousers they are corduroy
> Ditto my jacket and my vest;
> For I'm the wild and wooly boy,
> My name is Lummis; I'm the West!
>
> Who first beheld the Indian Race?
> Columbus, say you?
> I was the first to see his face;
> I've had him copyrighted too . . .[3]

In 1909, an editor of the Santa Fe Railway's effusive paean, *The Grand Canyon of Arizona: Being a Book of Words From Many Pens, About the Grand Canyon of the Colorado River in Arizona*, declared that Lummis's "most notable characteristic is his intense Americanism. He believes in

1

America for Americans. Knowing this great Southwest, he has always pleaded to have the tide of eager tourists turn toward it as an unmatched wonderland."[4] It was Lummis who coined the slogan, "See America First!"

Many responded to Lummis's call. The artists, writers, scientists, and railroad men who arrived in the Southwest at the dawn of the twentieth century shared an inspired view of the "magic region" they had discovered. Many were in retreat from the advancing mechanized, industrial world; others were in the avant-garde of pioneers forging new visions of America whose roots were in the Southwest. They found what they sought.

Ironically, it was the railroad's "streaks of rust"—the vanguard mechanical invaders from the East—that made the journey of discovery possible. It took them there and helped them stay. The railway's chief freight during its first decades was not the trappings of "civilization" it took into the heart of the Southwest, but its promise of a pristine, primitive Santa Fe Southwest. Many enthusiasts were mesmerized by the strangely exotic landscape and people they encountered. For them, the railway kept its promise while fulfilling its visions of, and for, America.

The relationship between artists and railway officials began even as the first locomotive penetrated into New Mexico from the north in 1879. Theirs was a communion of shared ideals and a collaboration of shared interests. The artists' quest was to paint the eternal sky while documenting the transient landscape and dying cultures. They were sympathetic but resigned to the fate of the region and its people. In the mid 1920s, D. H. Lawrence, then in New Mexico, lamented,

> But oh, let us have the grace and dignity to shelter these ancient centres of life, so that, if die they must, they die a natural death. And at the same time, let us try to adjust ourselves again to the Indian outlook, to take up an old dark thread from their vision, and see again as they see, without forgetting we are ourselves.[5]

The Pueblos' belief in the elemental unity of spirit in man, animal, and nature held particular appeal for many Anglo newcomers, and the harmony between the Indian and his environment was a frequent theme for Taos and Santa Fe painters and writers.[6]

The Power of Symbol

The region exerted a strong pull on the imaginations of the artists who migrated to the Southwest during the early years of the railroad; they were attracted by the simple expressions of existence they saw in the ritual lives of the Indians and Hispanics living in the landscape. Too, these artists were inspired by the call for an American art devoted to American subjects. In 1900, a Paris exhibition critic had concluded that ". . . there remains the somewhat depressing fact that [the exhibition's] works in the main are not national, do not exemplify American spirit or reflect American life.[7] Just twenty years later, a visiting reviewer reported that, "In that desert land a real school of American art has developed . . . ,"[8] freed from European models and influences.

The native cultures' art and magnificent surroundings were truly inspiring elements. Played out against this backdrop, the beneficial relationships between artists, their models, patrons, and communities created a congenial climate for energetic illumination of the Southwest experience.

The Santa Fe Railway executives, many themselves artists, writers, and scientists, nurtured a vivid conception of what the Southwest was—and what it could be—and found their visions reflected in the artists' paintings and the public's expectations. This bonded them in mutually held values that would be the basis for revolutionizing corporate advertising and the development of the first, and one of the most important, corporate art collections in the country.

This book is a story of visions and visionaries and how their powerful and poetic views shaped the Southwest—and opened it to our imaginations.

VISION of EMPIRE

FELLOW citizens, imagine, if you please, my right hand as Chicago, my left as St. Louis." Colonel Cyrus K. Holliday's voice wavered with emotion as he crossed his arms in front of his chest dramatically. "Eventually the railroad we contemplate will reach these two cities and, crossing at Topeka, the intersection of my arms, will extend to Galveston, the City of Mexico, and San Francisco." Holliday was exhorting a small group of prominent guests who had traveled by train that day in April 1869, along the first seven miles of track laid by the fledgling Atchison, Topeka & Santa Fe Railroad Company to share his dream. Holliday continued, "The coming tide of immigration will flow along these lines of railway, and like an ocean wave will advance up the sides of the Rockies and dash their foaming crests down upon the Pacific slope." A young man in the incredulous crowd fell to the ground laughing, and hooted, "Oh, the damned old fool!"[9]

The young man and the other skeptics who had laughed at Colonel Holliday were astounded when, by 1886, the Santa Fe Railroad had reached the Gulf of Mexico and the Pacific Ocean. Holliday, who had envisioned a great railroad that would follow the route of the Santa Fe Trail to Santa Fe and beyond, had been proven to be no fool, but a man of extraordinary vision. As a member of the Kansas Territorial Legislature, in 1859 Holliday had drafted the charter creating the railroad and lobbied it successfully through the legislature. When the company was organized the following year, he was elected first president.

It was against tremendous odds—including a relentless series of natural and man-made disasters in an atmosphere thick with violence and intrigue—that Holliday's prophetic vision became a magnificent reality.

By 1878, as the railroad track crept toward the Southwest, more or less following the Santa Fe Trail, its builders grew alarmed by the slow pace of construction. There was no time to lose. The best entrance into New Mexico was through Raton Pass, in the rugged mountains straddling the Colorado–New Mexico state line. As the Santa Fe track neared the pass, the company's arch rival, the Denver & Rio Grande Railroad, was laying track south toward the pass as rapidly as it could. The first railroad actually to begin construction there would receive the right of way.

The story of this race is the stuff of Wild West legends: the Santa Fe's chief locating engineer, disguised as a shepherd, explored the pass under the noses of the D&RG surveyors working there; D&RG officials intercepted a Santa Fe telegram revealing its plans to seize the pass; threats of gunplay between combative crews were frequent. These events were climaxed by the Santa Fe's frenzied scramble to be the first railroad to begin construction. The Santa Fe crew arrived at midnight, March 1, 1878, just hours ahead of the D&RG crew, and pressed revelers at a community dance into service. It must have been a discouraging, if humorous, sight that met the D&RG construction crew when they arrived to find men and women in party clothes wielding picks and shovels. Raton Pass belonged to the Santa Fe![10]

A decade after the Santa Fe Railroad had begun laying track in Topeka, its first locomotive crossed the summit of Raton Pass on the afternoon of December 7, 1878, climbing the mountain over a series of switchbacks. From then on, construction continued steadily southwest, toward Santa Fe.

From Triumph to Despair, and Back Again

The Railroad

The railroad is coming this way—
Let us go look at it near.
When we shall see it appear,
Ah, what a joy it will be.

Chorus: And when the tourists shall throng,
"Good morning!" I will repeat;
"Come in! Come in! I'll entreat,
"Come ye and list to my song!"

6

Up from the town on the line
Come running the Americanos,
Earning us everyone money —
Money for all us paisanos.

—New Mexican Folk Song[11]

The Santa Fe Railroad's dramatic entrance into New Mexico ushered in an era unimagined by the state's residents. Where the railroad went, enthusiasts saw nothing but prosperity ahead. The railroad replaced the slow, dangerous, and expensive Santa Fe Trail, bringing with it a steady wave of immigrants, abundant, inexpensive freight, and new opportunities for the bold adventurer and established resident. One orator who welcomed the railroad to Las Vegas, New Mexico, on July 4, 1879, called the Santa Fe a "great civilizer."

By 1887, the Atchison, Topeka & Santa Fe Railroad Company had become one of the greatest railroad systems in the world, extending from Lake Michigan to the Pacific

The Atchison, Topeka & Santa Fe Railway passing by Laguna Pueblo, New Mexico, ca. 1914. (Museum of New Mexico, neg. #149714.)

Ocean, from Denver to the Gulf of California, and from Kansas to the Gulf of Mexico; but its triumph almost destroyed the company.[12]

In 1888, the railroad's fortunes suffered a disastrous reversal. Bad crops, restrictive rate legislation, and tremendous competition from other railroads contributed to the company's plight. The Santa Fe replaced several of its directors and drastically cut fares and freight fees, but continued to buy more miles of track. An advertising executive writing in the 1920s of the Santa Fe's troubles remembered that "It slowly went to pieces. It neglected its property, defaulted its interest, entered receivership. It went down into the valley of the shadows. It became the butt of ridicule, the contempt of everyone. . . . 'That streak of rust across Kansas,' sneered a big New York banker, sometimes accused of real vision, 'I should as soon throw my money into a sewer as to think of buying a single share

of its stock.'"[13] The company succeeded in avoiding
bankruptcy, but in 1893, "when the English bankers . . .
refused further credit, the end had arrived." A U.S.
Circuit Court judge appointed receivers to run the company.[14] On January 1, 1896, the reorganized Atchison,
Topeka & Santa Fe Railway (changed from Railroad)
took over the remaining property of the former company.
Edward P. Ripley, a man himself with visionary ideas, was
elected president and began almost immediately to initiate
reforms that would lead the railroad rapidly to the
astounding success that Colonel Holliday had prophesied.
Through Ripley's efforts, Holliday was at last recognized
as "the dreamer, the enthusiast, the father of the
system, who early saw the golden future of the great
Southwest. . . . He it was who . . . foresaw the . . . vast system that was destined to transform the entire Southwest. . . . just exactly as he told his jeering neighbors it
would 'way back in the sixties."[15]

When Ripley retired as president of the railroad in 1920,
he had built one of the greatest railroads in the world and
had endowed it with a reputation for providing the highest
standards of service. In a 1915 speech, Ripley praised
those who had worked with him to rehabilitate the railroad and restore its reputation. "[N]o more able and
efficient men are in existence," he exclaimed. "No one man
is of any possible consequence; no one man can accom-
plish anything in a large way without loyal and enthusiastic support. . . . The esprit de corps of the Santa Fe has
become known and is commented on by everybody everywhere . . . if I have lived to win the approbation of my con-
temporaries . . . I can look with complacency on the signs
of the closing day and go to my rest content."[16]

The Titan of Chasms

In 1895, the year before Ripley became the Santa Fe's
president, W. F. White, then traffic manager of the road,
had begun studying the possibilities of advertising for the
struggling railroad. Other railroads had already begun to
advertise their lines. The Rock Island line was "putting
out the ingenious miniature Rogers statuettes of the traveler in the linen duster confronting the great map of the
pioneer railroad . . . ; the Chicago & Alton was populariz-
ing the phrase, 'The Only Way.'"[17]

Ripley was at heart a promoter. He encouraged White to
develop an advertising campaign as clever as the statuette
and as colorful as the Chicago & Alton's red-and-black
Alton Limited. White soon "hit upon the great painting of
the Grand Cañon which Thomas Moran had just completed. . . . The road bought all the rights to the Moran
picture and had very careful lithographic reprints made of

it. These it framed in handsome gilt frames and then sent them out, first by the hundreds and then by the thousands. It placed them in offices, in hotels, in schools, even in homes—almost anywhere that there was a fair chance of the picture bringing in business."[18]

The Santa Fe had done more than "hit upon" Moran's painting of the Grand Canyon; in 1892 it invited him to travel there at its expense to paint, in return for the copyright to one painting of its choice to use in its advertising campaign. Moran's visit occurred almost twenty years after his first trip there with Major John Wesley Powell, who was surveying the Grand Canyon of the Colorado. Moran had stood at its rim, "astonished at the majestic spectacle before him. It was, he said, 'by far the most awfully grand and impressive scene that I have ever yet seen.'"[19]

Thomas Moran and daughters at the Grand Canyon. (Museum of New Mexico, neg. #149714.)

The railway selected for its use one of the most inspired images of the Grand Canyon that Moran ever created.

Moran's 1892 trip to the Grand Canyon from Flagstaff had been a difficult and uncomfortable ride by stagecoach. Within a few years, realizing the canyon's tourist possibilities, the Santa Fe purchased a bankrupt line and extended it to the south rim of the canyon. It was a momentous

Locomotive 282 arrives at North Rim of the Grand Canyon, September 18, 1901. (Courtesy of the Santa Fe Railway.)

occasion when on September 18, 1901, "Santa Fe engineer Harry Schlee eases locomotive 282 along the last mile of track. Though his passengers are anxious to arrive, he pulls the heavy load of tank cars cautiously over the new rails. The few passengers talk excitedly about the event soon to occur. In minutes, they will be the first visitors to reach the Grand Canyon by train. . . . Harry Schlee sounds the whistle as 282 pulls up to the station—the end of the line and the beginning of an era."[20]

In what would prove to be one of his most visionary—and profitable—acts as president of the Santa Fe Railway, in 1900 Ripley promoted William Haskell Simpson (1858–1933)—a natural advertising genius who was a clerk in the general passenger department—to be the railway's general advertising agent. With the spur line to the Grand Canyon in operation, Simpson began to send other artists on three-to-four week excursions there to capture its awesome grandeur on canvas. These annual visits produced numerous paintings, drawings, and lithographs for museums, magazines, and books, all glorifying the majesty of the West, the railway, and the food and lodging provided by Fred Harvey.

Fred Harvey: The Man Who Civilized the West

"Well, Fred Harvey . . . he revolutionized the railroad eating house in the West. He made it possible for persons to get the very best of eating from Chicago to the coast, to get it at any hour of day or night, to have it served in the very best style, and all for the smallest possible outlay of coin; and, besides this, he furnished pretty and useful wives for no man knows how many sighing swains, and he raised the standard of living for half a continent. . . ."[21]

Ripley's selection of Fred Harvey to develop and run the railway's food service and hotel accommodations was another inspired collaboration. Before they joined forces, meals in railway stations "consisted of rancid bacon, canned beans, or three kinds of eggs—eggs from the East aged and preserved in lime, ranch eggs from local farms, and yard eggs laid near the depot. The soda biscuits served with the eggs were known as 'sinkers' by the patrons. Diners could choose either cold tea or bitter black coffee to accompany their meal. The tables lacked napkins and were covered by dirty cloths on which were placed chipped and broken crockery by the 'hash slingers' who waited on the customers in the 'dining room.'"[22] Routinely the waiters would serve the meal in the last few seconds of the twenty-minute stop, just as the train whistled its departure. The hungry passenger would race back to the train, leaving the uneaten food to be served to another traveler; the train crew and waiters split the profits made on this scheme to recycle food. Rather than attempt a meal during these short stops, many travelers would instead dash to the local saloon, usually the most comfortable place around, and throw down several drinks before boarding again.[23]

Little is known of Frederick Henry Harvey (1835–1901) before his immigration from London to New York when he was fifteen. The story goes that, like many other successful frontier entrepreneurs, Harvey arrived in New York an inexperienced young man with only ten dollars in his pocket.

He found a job busing in a cafe for the meager salary of two dollars a week. Dissatisfied, he drifted south to New Orleans, then west to St. Louis, where he entered the restaurant business in 1856. He later lost everything he'd made through the treachery of his business partner, who absconded with their funds. Harvey and his young wife

A Harvey House lunchroom counter, Vaughn, New Mexico, 1901. (Kansas State Historical Society.)

went to Leavenworth, Kansas, where Harvey found work as general western freight agent for the Chicago, Burlington & Quincy Railroad. His travels for the CB&Q exposed him to vile food and filthy sleeping quarters, at exorbitant prices. He believed it would be profitable to provide good food and clean, comfortable hotels to railroad travelers. In 1876, he persuaded a Santa Fe Railway official that the idea was worth a try, and they struck a "gentlemen's agreement" that Harvey would run the lunch counter in the Topeka station. His lunchroom, with its clean, white linens, china dishes, gleaming silver, and tasty food was so successful that company officials urged him to take over operation of the railway's restaurant and hotel in Florence, Kansas. Harvey refurnished the hotel and recruited a chef from Chicago's Palmer House to be manager. Now "tourists could continue their tours without first outfitting a medicine chest and adding to their life insurance, and sojourners could sojourn without whole families of the *cimex lictularius* (also known as the genus *bedbugus*) holding carousels at the wayfarer's expense."[24]

From the beginning, Harvey also had high expectations of his customers. For instance, he required men to wear coats in the dining rooms (a rule which was challenged but upheld in 1924 by an Oklahoma Supreme Court, which ruled, ". . . those unwilling momentarily to endure a slight discomfort, out of regard for the feelings, tastes and desires of others, are few compared with the storm of protests the abrogation of the rule would ultimately produce").[25]

Nevertheless, the customer was always right. Harvey once told a disgruntled employee, "Of course he is a crank . . . but we must please him. It is our business to please cranks, for anyone can please a gentleman."[26]

Maintain the Standard, Regardless of Cost

"[T]he Harvey service was peculiarly adapted to the Santa Fe and the Santa Fe was peculiarly adapted to the Harvey service. They had developed together, both under broad, liberal management. Sometimes the question is asked, 'Why is it not possible to have similarly wonderful dining and hotel accommodations on some other railroad?' The answer is simple: There is but one Santa Fe."[27]

Harvey's success was measured by the number of passengers the Harvey Houses attracted; profit margin was secondary. The railway's employees gave their enthusiastic support to his efforts to sustain exceptional standards. As the Santa Fe sped across the desert transporting passengers—and the food, furnishings, and materials for the Harvey dining rooms and resorts—a trainman would learn how many passengers wanted a meal and then wire the count ahead to the next stop. When the train was a mile from its destination, the engineer would blow the whistle, the uniformed Harvey train attendant stationed on the platform would ring a gong, and the expectant Harvey Girls—the waitresses—would serve the first course. Passengers poured into the immaculate lunchrooms to plates of steaming food on the tables. Drink orders were taken and cups placed either up, down, or tilted to signify whether the customer wanted coffee, tea, or milk. Customers leisurely ate their meals.

More than 100,000 Harvey Girls worked for the Harvey operation between 1883 and the late 1950s. Harvey recruited these intelligent, attractive, refined, and educated (at least to the eighth grade) young women through ads in newspapers east of the Mississippi. The women responded to the ads mostly for economic reasons, but also for the adventure, travel, and the possibility of marriage to

exciting men they hoped to meet in the West. Their start-
ing salary was $17.50 a week, plus tips, room and board,
and vacations home.[28] After receiving intensive training,
the women were assigned throughout the system. While
under contract, they lived in dormitories supervised by
matrons, were forbidden to marry for at least a year, and
had to follow strict house rules. One former Harvey Girl
recalled, "Oh, yes, we had rules. You had better get in
before a specified hour or the back door was locked. Some
girls would try to climb over the fence to get in on time."[29]
Despite rules and chaperones, thousands of Harvey Girls
married ranchers, miners, merchants, cowboys, and railroad men, and thousands named their firstborn sons after
Fred Harvey. Will Rogers once said Fred Harvey "kept
the West in food and wives."[30]

A Santa Fe publication reported. "The service is perfect.
. . . At Fred Harvey's you are always expected. The girls
are ever in their best bib and tucker, spotlessly gowned,
manicured, groomed, combed, dental-flossed—bright,
healthy, intelligent girls—girls that are never flip nor
fresh, but who give you the attention that never obtrudes,
but which is hearty and heartfelt."[31]

Harvey Houses were elaborate, luxurious hotels

designed in the Southwest or California Spanish-Mission style. Once again, it was Santa Fe president Ripley's inspired idea to use these architectural styles, particularly the "Santa Fe Style."[32]

Although not in the "Santa Fe style," one of the first and most extravagant hotels the Santa Fe built was the Montezuma, near Las Vegas, New Mexico. Constructed in 1882, it was named after the Aztec ruler who was said to have bathed in the resort's hot springs. The railroad built a spur line from the Las Vegas depot to the mineral waters and asked Harvey to develop the resort.[33]

Standing in a picturesque canyon, the four-story wood frame Queen Anne style hotel was crowned by an eight-story tower. Each of the 270 guest rooms had balconies ". . . for those whose mood it may be not to climb, or walk, or ride burros, whose youth and spirits have been tamed, or who sagely know that what they get from that balcony long and wide, and without exertion, is quite enough. The sunshine falls in wide sheets there all day. . . ."[34] The resort offered "cures" with its hot mineral waters which, ". . . aside from any medicinal properties . . . are cosmetic in their action upon the skin, and have an effect not to be obtained by any formula thus far patented. The skin is given a velvety and pliable texture delightful to feminine visitors."[35]

The Montezuma became a major destination, with four

Navajos greeting the train at El Tovar Hotel, Grand Canyon. (Courtesy of the Santa Fe Railway.)

trains carrying passengers to the site every day.[36] It burned to the ground in 1884; the hotel that replaced it, poetically called the Phoenix, was sold after El Tovar Hotel, built in 1905 at the south rim of the Grand Canyon, became the more popular stop along the route.

El Tovar, "a long, low, rambling structure" built of pine logs and Douglas fir, was described as being "in complete harmony with the surroundings — on one side the mighty gorge, on the other, the Coconino Forest, the whole

El Tovar Rendezvous Room, 1905. (Kansas State Historical Society.)

expressing a quiet dignity and unassuming luxury. . . . Seven miles away by trail, and a mile if measured straight downward, is the Colorado River, its tumult never reaching the upper stillness. . . . There are spacious sheltered and open verandas . . . roof gardens . . . sunshine . . . invigorating mountain air. . . . Everywhere a riot of color and beauty of form—a vision unspeakable."[37] The resort featured a clubhouse with billiard and pool tables, a rendezvous or lounging room "with huge stone fireplaces and decorated with trophies of the chase . . . ," a solarium, a music-room, and a dining room constructed to look like a Norwegian great hall, with a rough-board overhead ceiling and huge, long trusses that created a rustic but elegant

space. Several art galleries were "devoted to the sale of paintings and photographs. On the wall hang paintings of Southwest scenery from the brushes of noted American artists, perhaps including one of Thomas Moran's masterpieces, also canvases by Sauerwein, Couse, Sharp, Leigh, Jorgenson, Burgdorff, Wachtel, and Rollins."[38]

Simpson's Solution

"Any man who is really an artist will find the Southwest . . . a region where the ingenuity, the imagination, and the love of God are . . . visible at every turn. . . . It is high time for the artists to come upon the Southwest."

—Charles F. Lummis [39]

And, come they did. When Simpson had joined the Santa Fe Railway in 1881, its advertising effort was unso-phisticated. A Santa Fe folder "loudly proclaimed our line to be 'The Gold Hunters,' 'Buffalo Hunters' and 'Home Seekers' Road!' and went on to prove the statement with humorous woodcuts and a tongue-twisting flow of hyperbole that would have done credit to P. T. Barnum." Determined to change the company's image while promoting tourism to the Southwest and ensuring prosperity for the line, Simpson

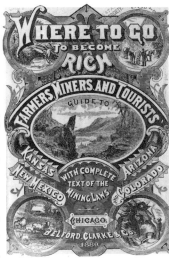

16

arranged many trips to the Grand Canyon for artists in exchange for paintings suitable for promotional campaigns. "If Will Simpson should ever set about to write a book on 'Artists I Have Toted to the Hopi House and Back,' it probably would speedily become recognized as the 'Who's Who' of that profession . . . ," a writer exclaimed.[40]

His revolutionary promotion centered on paintings of the "Santa Fe Southwest"—primarily portraits of Indians, landscapes, and genre scenes—by talented artists who, inspired by their quest for the romantic southwestern subject, were painting the region in a manner that greatly appealed to Simpson. He looked for brilliant colors and a romantic realism in the pictures. Rather than continue to purchase only the one-time use of a painting, he urged that the Santa Fe buy them, to avoid problems with reproduction rights later on. "The railway's management agreed, and gave Simpson authority to purchase, sell, trade, and use such paintings as needed for advertising and decoration."[41]

In 1903, Simpson purchased Bertha Menzler Dressler's (1871–1947) painting, *San Francisco Peaks,* the first work in a collection that would grow to include more than 600 paintings. Dressler and her painter husband had traveled to northern Arizona as early as 1900 to make sketches on the Navajo Reservation. *San Francisco Peaks* probably was painted during that trip; Simpson may have seen the painting in Arizona or in Chicago, at Dressler's home. After graduating from the Chicago Art Institute in 1892 and studying in Paris for several years, she had returned to Chicago to paint portraits, turning to landscapes only after the 1903 trip to Arizona. Inspired by the scenery and Simpson's support, Dressler returned frequently and gained an excellent reputation for her desert and Grand Canyon scenes. In a *Chicago Times Herald* article, she was described as being "possessed of imagination and not a little poetic feeling. Her landscapes are charming. Her touch is true, her eye musical. . . ."[42]

Indian-Detour advertisement. (Museum of New Mexico, neg. #16409. Photograph by Ben Wittick.)

Simpson moved swiftly to take advantage of the mood of the country. In 1907, he acquired 108 paintings. The romantic movement in literature and art was "still fresh in the minds of Americans," and in the West the romance was still alive. Many longed nostalgically for a return to the imagined past. The Santa Fe Railway was in an excellent position to benefit from this sentiment. "Among all the publicists of the region, the railroads were without rivals in their ability to bring the West into the living rooms of the American people with special attention given to its cultural and topographical significance."[43]

Most of the works were used in an advertising campaign astounding in its breadth: "Its lithographs, its posters, its superb annual calendars, its advertising pictures of every sort, even the great New Mexican colonies of artists that it has helped upbuild in recent years both at Taos and at Santa Fe, are by no means the end of its art endeavors. It

Oraibi Pueblo, Hopi Arizona, ca. 1890. (Museum of New Mexico, neg. #16409.)

has made a large feature of lantern slides and of films that it both loans and gives to travel lecturers. It places these in schools and universities. . . . Seventy-five colored slides and from a thousand to two thousand feet of motion picture films, all in a neat case, form an assistance that any travel lecturer greatly appreciates."[44] The Santa Fe never worried unduly about promotional costs. "It is reasonably careful about the expenditures and beyond that it fixes its eyes upon the results—and nothing else. Results count."[45]

In the process, Simpson became an admirer and

Louis Akin painting at the Rim of the Grand Canyon, ca. 1905–06. (Museum of Northern Arizona.)

important patron of art. The railroad gave his collecting its full support, motivated partly by its hope for greater profits, partly to achieve greater recognition and prestige.

Simpson sought out artists who would paint the images he wanted in the Santa Fe collection. In 1903, he offered New York artist Louis Akin (1868–1913) transportation to Arizona in exchange for a commitment to paint the Hopi Indians. Akin accepted the offer eagerly. He arrived in Arizona that September "emotionally depressed, despairing of city life in New York, and resolved to find himself by living among the Hopi Indians."[46] For many months he lived at the Moqui pueblo of Oraibi in a rented room and began quietly to participate in the community, learning the language and dressing in the Indian manner. "[A]fter he had lived with the Hopi a year or so, he was initiated into one of the secret societies of the young Hopi men, danced with them in their underground lodgeroom, the kiva, and ran with them on their visits to their neighboring villages."[47] "It is simply too good to leave," he wrote. "It's the best stuff in America and has scarcely been touched." He did return to New York, but in 1906 was back in Flagstaff and for the rest of his life painted the Arizona Indians and the Grand Canyon.

Simpson commissioned his 1907 painting, *El Tovar Hotel, Grand Canyon*. "[I]t must have met Santa Fe's highest expectations. El Tovar fills the left background, its warm, rustic facade partly obscured by piñon pine. . . . To the right, the brink of the Canyon drops off and opens out in

Buffalo Dance, First Mesa, Hopi, ca. 1911. (Museum of New Mexico, neg. #36872. Photograph by H. F. Robinson.)

an array of mid-morning pastels. . . . Combining a powerful view of the Canyon with an unobtrusive impression of El Tovar, the picture is considerably more than just commercial art."[48]

Most artists who went to the Southwest for the railway found it a "painter's Mecca." Frank Paul Sauerwein (1871–1910), who suffered from tuberculosis for the last twenty years of his life, went there in 1891 for the climate but stayed because he grew to love the desert. The railroad reproduced his painting *The First Santa Fe Train Crossing the Desert* on a postcard. Sauerwein viewed painting at the Grand Canyon as a great economic advantage for an artist. "At the Grand Canyon," he wrote, "I had the good fortune to sell two little canvases. . . . If it could be materialized, there would be the ideal place for a studio, from every point of view. . . . At the point where the railroad touches the Canyon . . . practically every tourist that crosses the continent stops for a day or more. . . . Every one of the thousands who go there would see my pictures. . . . It is a place of such immense possibilities that I shall bend every effort toward getting an entering wedge in there."[49] In 1905, the Fred Harvey organization agreed to sell his paintings at El Tovar.

Like Akin, Sauerwein enjoyed close relations with the Hopi. An English tourist who met him in 1903 wrote: ". . . what he loved was to wander among the Indians of Arizona and New Mexico. His sketches, both of the scenery and of the natives, were the best I have ever seen. He knew the Indians well. They had allowed him to come down into the kiva or sacred chamber with them among the snakes. I do not know if he was initiated into the Hopi snake clan, but he was qualified for it."[50] After his death at the age of thirty-nine, his ashes were scattered on the Painted Desert of Arizona.

The Santa Fe and Taos Art Colonies: Far Off the Beaten Track

Simpson acquired most of the paintings for the collection from Taos and Santa Fe artists who had settled there to paint uniquely southwestern icons: exotic natives and fantastic landscape. These artists had responded to the prevalent sentiment, captured in Charles Lummis's call to "See America First." "My hope is growing that I shall live to see Americans proud of knowing America, and ashamed not to know it," Lummis wrote. "If we would cease to depend so much upon other countries for our standards of life and thought, we would have taken the first step toward an Americanism which would certainly be becoming and patriotic."[51]

Thomas Moran joined in urging artists to paint American subjects. "It has often occurred to me as a curious and anomalous fact," he wrote, "that American artists are prone to seek the subjects for their art in foreign lands, to the almost entire exclusion of their own. . . . That there is a nationalism in art needs no proof. It is bred from a knowledge of and sympathy with their surroundings, and no foreigner can imbue himself with the spirit of a country not his own. Therefore he should paint his own land."[52]

Although Charles Craig (1846–1931), in 1881, was the

first Anglo artist to work in Taos, and artist-illustrator Joseph Sharp (1859–1953), known as the "father" of the Taos colony, visited there in 1893 seeking Indian subject matter, it actually was begun in 1898 by Ernest L. Blumenschein (1874–1960) and Bert Geer Phillips (1868–1956) when, during a painting expedition through New Mexico, a broken wagon wheel landed them in Taos. Blumenschein later wrote, "It had to end in the Taos valley, green with trees and fields of alfalfa, populated by dark skinned people who greeted me pleasantly. Then I saw my first Taos Indians, picturesque, colorful, dressed in blankets artistically draped. New Mexico had gripped me—and I was not long in deciding that if Phillips would agree with me, if he felt as inspired to work as I, the Taos valley and its surrounding magnificent country would be

Taos Pueblo, ca. 1892. (Photograph by Bert Geer Phillips. Kit Carson Historic Museums.)

the end of our wagon trip. Mexico and other lands unknown could wait until the future."[53]

In 1907, Simpson bought three paintings from Phillips, all portraits of Taos Indians. It was also that year that Simpson initiated the famous Santa Fe Railway calendar. To be chosen as a calendar artist was a significant honor—the painting selected for the calendar would soon appear on the walls of 300,000 homes, schools, and offices. Few artists could have imagined such recognition; most were eager to respond to this unique opportunity.

In 1914, the romantic painting *Wal-si-see—Good Medicine*, by E. Irving Couse (1866–1936), appeared on the calendar, the first of twenty-three paintings by him that would decorate the calendars. Couse, who had arrived in Taos in 1902, devoted his efforts almost entirely to painting the subtleties of the Indians' "smooth flesh, tense muscles, and fine bone structure."[54] The portraits were idealized images of Indian men. "The physical beauty of the Taos Indian men delighted Couse," wrote Virginia Couse Leavitt. "He . . . picked the most classically ideal types to model for him and painted them with stunning accuracy. . . . His depictions of Indians engaged in craft, ritual or hunting activities were always metaphors for the Native American

21

perspective of life, which is inextricably intertwined with their religious view of the world. . . . His Indians, contemplative and timeless, are in constant communion with the spiritual universe that guides their every action."[55] Taos Indian Ben Luhan modeled for Couse for "as long as the painter lived and came to be known as Ben 'Couse' Luhan. After working as model all morning Ben served as gardener for Mrs. Couse in the afternoons."[56]

Couse and Simpson exchanged ideas freely during the creation of the calendar paintings. Couse wrote to Simpson, "I made this sketch light & snappy with a light background in order to depart somewhat from the similarity of previous calendars nearly all of which have had a dark background. I would be pleased to know your views of this sketch & whatever criticism you may have to make."[57] In response to Couse's sketch for *Grinding Corn*, Simpson commented, "It would seem that the olla, the metate, the buckskin leggins [sic] on the man and his head dress afford special opportunity for the brilliant white effect mentioned in previous correspondence. The strong white gives a sparkle to the picture, which is very attractive for calendar use." While they were working on *Indian Flute Player* for the 1933 calendar, Simpson suggested "a trifle lighter background. The left knee of the figure on the right, seems a bit out of line—however, my glasses may be twisted—anyway, do as you think best. Note what you say about the green leggings on the boy. Perhaps the green should be toned down a bit, but your good taste will decide that."[58]

By 1937, Simpson may have tired of Couse's squatting Indian: "While we are on the subject of calendar pictures, wish you would submit two or three sketches as suggestions for the 1937 calendar. Would like to hold the figures as big as possible, and in view of the series, think the picture should contain not more than two, and these should not be in a "squatting" posture. There is

Sketches by E. Irving Couse for The Chief. *(Couse Family Archives, Couse Enterprises, Ltd.)*

plenty of time to work out something especially good."[59]

Simpson realized that strong visual images of the southwestern landscape and its indigenous residents would attract tourists to the region. He wanted the Santa Fe to be the line to take them there. Intending to synthesize the image of the Indian with that of the railway, he designed the calendars to carry that subliminal message, a masterful ploy in corporate image-making. "'The Santa Fe Indian,' who dominated the calendar, came into being. This Indian possessed an aura of glamour. An intangibility. An ineffable essence. The idea was to present a radiant image of Indian life."[60]

Couse was one of many artists who approached the subject of the southwestern Indians romantically. By the end of the nineteenth century, the public's perception of the American Indian had changed from that of a "degraded race of savage people who were out of step with the modern world,"[61] to a highly romanticized image, one in which the noble, spiritual qualities of the Indian were emphasized. This new perception was fostered in part by the numerous fairs and expositions held in Chicago, New Orleans, and Philadelphia at the turn of the century, which introduced native culture to the general American public, and in part through the promotion of southwestern archaeology and anthropology by Edgar L. Hewett, who in 1909 founded and directed the School of American Archaeology and the Museum of New Mexico in Santa Fe.

Artists' concerns for what they perceived as the demise of the American Indian also contributed to the public's changing perceptions. Inspired by the writing of James Fenimore Cooper and the paintings of George Catlin, artistic images of the "vanishing" Indian became ubiquitous. These expressions were an odd combination of the romantic impulse and realistic ethnography. Of course, these were the outsider whites' perceptions and quickly became stereotypical.

E. Martin Hennings (1886–1956), a member of the Taos Society of Artists, a promotional group formed by several Taos artists in 1915 to exhibit and sell their paintings around the country, portrayed the Indians as dignified and heroic people riding peacefully through golden aspens or sage-covered deserts or pausing briefly by mountain streams. His daughter, Helen Hennings Winton, wrote, "[H]e was a gentle man, kind and compassionate, with an unending supply of patience. His work illustrates his

calmness of spirit, his oneness with nature."[62] Hennings perceived in the Taos Indians these same qualities and was attracted to them.

In Taos, Walter Ufer (1876–1936) became a plein air artist whose paintings were noted for their light, bright palette. He said, "I choose my motifs and take my models to my motifs. I design the painting there. I do not make any small sketches of my models first, but put my full vitality and enthusiasm into the one and original painting."[63] Ufer felt that the traditions of the American Indian were fast disappearing under the pressure of "Americanization." "The Indian has lost his race pride. . . . He wants only to be American. Our civilization has terrific power. We don't feel it, but that man out there in the mountains feels it, and he cannot cope with such pressure. . . ."[64]

Ufer and other artists tried to portray an accurate image of the Indian, but their work was imbued with lingering traces of romanticism—they could not abandon the idea of the American Indian as the quintessential symbol of the New World and the wilderness. The romantic movement emphasized intuition over intellect and the dramatic over the mundane. So, even in their so-called genre scenes, the Indian was idealized. References to pristine nature and the legendary past were frequently present in the painters' imagery. This view fit precisely with Simpson's promotional ideas, and his support brought recognition to the Taos and Santa Fe artists as creators present at the source.

In Santa Fe, Warren E. Rollins (1861–1962) became known as the "dean of the Santa Fe art colony." He had traveled in Hopi country between 1900 and 1906, painting

Meeting the train to sell pottery, Pueblo of Laguna, New Mexico, 1902. (Kansas State Historical Society.)

poetic renditions of Hopi myths, legends, and ceremonial rites for which he won great acclaim. "It is evident that the lore and mystique of these ancient people were far more appealing to the artists than the actual scenes he sketched around the pueblos."[65] He exhibited his works at Santa Fe's historic old Palace of the Governors before 1910.

William Penhallow Henderson (1877–1943) moved to Santa Fe in 1916 with his wife, prominent poet Alice Corbin. Henderson was one of the few artists with work in the Santa Fe art collection to devote his attention to Hispanic, rather than Indian, traditions. In Santa Fe he developed his reputation as a master colorist. "The pastels of Santa Fe are pure fantasy to those who are unfamiliar

Acoma Pueblo. (Kansas State Historical Society.)

with the area. The hills cannot be that rounded, the trees cannot be of such fine shape or color, the adobe houses and walls cannot be of such color and texture, and the people cannot be so picturesque. And yet these things are all true . . . to those who know this land and have the eye of the artist or the poet to see them."[66]

Through the years, Gerald Cassidy's (1879–1934) paintings were reproduced primarily on postcards and posters that were shown and sold on the Santa Fe's trains and in

La Fonda, ca. 1920s. (The Robert Clarkson Collection #37725, New Mexico State Records Center and Archives.)

its hotels from Chicago to California. Of those posters, ten framed originals are still on exhibit at the La Fonda Hotel in Santa Fe.

Destinations and Detours

La Fonda, located literally at the end of the Old Santa Fe Trail, was purchased by the railway in 1925 and run by Fred Harvey. Harvey commissioned architect and interior designer Mary E. J. Colter to create atmospheres in La Fonda and other Harvey Houses evocative of southwestern ambience and traditions. "With their long portales and intimate patios, their floors covered with Navaho blankets, their walls hung with Spanish santos and retablos or painted with mural reproductions of Navaho sandpaintings, their great fireplaces smoking with piñon . . . their news-stands full of the finest books, photographs, and monographs on the region, their curio cases of Navaho and Zuñi silver, Pueblo pottery, and Apache baskets . . . their hotel rooms with their cool, clean beds—the Harvey House was not only a haven

La Fonda Interior, 1902–1948. (Courtesy of La Fonda Archives.)

in the wilderness, but an institution that had no parallel in America. Perhaps more than any single organization, the Fred Harvey system introduced America to Americans."[67]

Colter designed interiors for many Harvey hotels,

including El Ortiz, at Lamy, El Navajo, at Gallup, and La Posada, at Winslow. Among her most important commissions was the Indian Building at the Alvarado Hotel in Albuquerque, constructed in California Spanish-Mission style. "One of the most beautiful and Harvey's largest hotel, it was built along the track in 1903 and named after an early explorer of the Southwest. It had acres of landscaped grounds with lawns, walks, shade trees, shrubs, hedges, flowers, fountains with goldfish and turtles, sun parlors—in every respect refreshing—a wonderful welcome to the West."[68] The Indian Building, next to the hotel and railway station, displayed outstanding examples of Spanish, Mexican, and Native American antiques and crafts in a museum setting, although most items were for sale. The gift shop's success was assured; to them, architect-designer Colter brought flair and imagination, Fred Harvey's son-in-law, John F. Huckel, brought business acumen, and Herman Schweizer, Harvey's curio shop manager, brought keen judgment and the reputation as one of the country's best judges of Indian and Spanish art. To entice tourists as they stepped off the train onto the platform in front of the Indian Building, were "live Indians" selling their wares along the walk leading to the building's entrance. One Harvey ad read: "See patient Navajo squaws weaving blankets, their men engaged in fashioning showy bracelets, rings, and trinkets. . . . Undisturbed by the eager tourist, the stoic works on as unconcernedly as though in his reservation home."[69]

As the Santa Fe and the Harvey Company "began systematically to promote mass production of crafts . . . a dramatic shift took place—away from the tradition . . . to an arts-and-crafts industry geared to the parlor tastes of the East. . . . The new arts-and-crafts industry provided financial assistance to needy native communities and notoriety to some Indian artisans. It brought . . . a new awareness of native crafts to collectors of Southwestern art and to

tourists and it appealed to American nationalism. Furthermore, the promotion of Indian 'artifacts' by Fred Harvey and the Santa Fe Railway enhanced their prestige and business flourished."[70] "Harvey purchased only rugs of the highest quality. . . . Over the years, thousands of textiles were purchased from reservation traders to stock Harvey Stores. Harvey thwarted efforts to produce factory-made 'Navajo' rugs. To ensure a continued market, high prices, and limited sales outlets for 'genuine' Navajo rugs," Harvey bought the machine-made rugs and displayed them prominently in his shops, labeled as imitations.[71]

Colter also designed the Hopi House at the Grand Canyon, built by "Hopi workmen using the same structural design found in prehistoric pueblos, and decorated by Hopi artists. Two days before it was opened the Hopis held a dedication ceremony. She was the only White invited."[72] The Hopi House symbolized "the partnership between commercialism and romanticism that typified so much of Fred Harvey architecture."[73] "She designed not replicas of these earlier buildings, but recreations, buildings that captured the essence of the past. . . . Mary Colter was more interested in rediscovering the cultural heritage

The Harvey House, El Ortiz, Lamy, New Mexico, ca. 1920s. (Kansas State Historical Society.)

of the region than in imitating European styles. Her buildings fit their setting because they grew out of the history of the land. They belonged."[74]

La Fonda, in Santa Fe, also served as headquarters for the Indian-Detours, which offered the "detourist" or "dude" one-to-three-day tours "to the cliff dwellings at El Rito de Frijoles," or to San Ildefonso Pueblo where "we shall see the primitive methods of manufacturing the famous black pottery," or to Puye, where "everywhere on the open upland above are evidences of the Forgotten People," or Taos, a "mecca for artists of national and international reputation."[75] Tours were also offered to Carlsbad Caverns and the Painted Desert. The "couriers," well-educated young women guides, were hired and trained by Erna Fergusson, a well-known southwestern author who had run her own tour business, Koshare Tours, before joining the Harvey system.

Organized in 1926, the Indian Detours carried detourists into the unknown. Like the Harvey Girls, couriers were given "cram courses in the geology, archaeology, history, and flora and fauna of the Southwest," according to former courier Beatrice Chauvenet. "I read books and attended evening lectures given for Detour guests at La Fonda by specialists. . . . By day I went along as a

courier-in-training on the regular three-day Detour. . . . We ran an overnight trip to Taos where we visited the pueblo and many artists' studios. We were welcomed by Bert Phillips, Irving Couse, Ernest Blumenschein, Joseph Henry Sharp, among others."[76]

Titan of Chasms

"Dear Mr. Moran: Am glad your feet are soon to turn Arizonaward. Feel quite sure Mr. Harvey will be glad to extend the usual courtesies at El Tovar. Am writing him to-day with reference to that; also your need for a studio. The special studio building talked of the last time you were at the Canyon has been side-tracked for awhile, account retrenchment. Should think room might be found in the Hopi House, however. . . . Very sincerely, W. H. Simpson, Advertising Agent."[77] Not all of Simpson's artists were content to remain at work in the Taos and Santa Fe art colonies; many preferred the dramatic scenery of the Grand Canyon and its environs. Warren Rollins was one of them; he spent a great deal of time at the canyon, where the Santa Fe Railway provided him with a studio near El Tovar, "so he could interpret its vastness for the road's travel posters."[78]

Other artists also took advantage of studio space offered by the Santa Fe at the canyon's rim. In 1910, Simpson

Navajos working in La Fonda. (Courtesy La Fonda Archives.)

Hopi House, Grand Canyon. (Kansas State Historical Society.)

Indian-Detour map. (Courtesy of the Santa Fe Railway.)

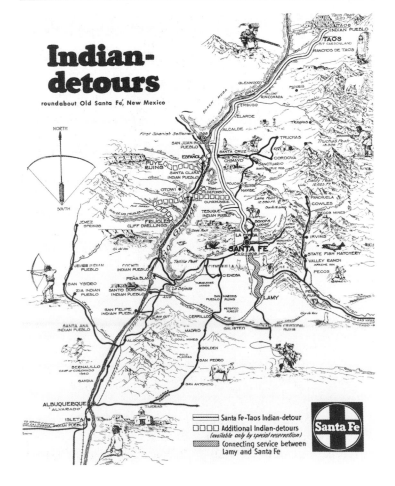

invited five prominent artists, including Thomas Moran, Elliott Daingerfield (1859–1932), and Edward H. Potthast (1857–1927), to travel to the Grand Canyon to paint its glories. "This Western jaunt represents an early instance of corporate patronization of the arts for it was financed by the Atchison, Topeka and Santa Fe Railways [sic]. . . . 'Never before had so large a group of serious

artists made such a pilgrimage to the Far West with the avowed intention of studying a given point of their own country, and thus will this visit to the Canyon become historical. . . . The painters worked all day and sometimes half the night, wandering far upon the rim in search of ivory cliffs, characteristic trees and bits of composition . . . Mr. Potthast worked indefatigably with brush and pencil and took back numerous interesting sketches.' "[79]

"The trip had an especially efficacious and expansive effect on Potthast's art. . . . The Canyon landscapes are among his more original and significant accomplishments. . . . The jewellike tones of [a painting] inscribed 'to my friend W. H. Simpson' exhibit the artist's rich and masterly control of impressionistic color."[80] Potthast was a prolific painter but his own severest critic. "During all these years of our friendship," his art dealer recalled, "I

have never heard him praise even his best work. . . . I doubt whether he ever has felt that he has produced a finished picture."[81] Elliott Daingerfield was most famous for his paintings of the Grand Canyon; he was called the "genius of the Canyon" after one of his best-loved canyon works. Of that painting, a critic said, "If it were in a rail-

road station, crowds would miss their trains. Poets have written to it. Its sweetness, its grandiloquence, its coloring (for it has coloring, not color) make it the very ideal for those who do not see a painting, but feel it through the haze of sentimentality."[82]

In 1906, the "Sagebrush Rembrandt," William R. Leigh (1866–1955), persuaded Simpson to provide him with a trip to the West in return for a painting. "The West lived up to Leigh's highest expectations. His life and his art took on new definition and purpose. . . . Leigh's style so suited Simpson that the Santa Fe Railway purchased not one but five paintings to hang in the two lodges at the Grand Canyon."[83] When he received Leigh's photographs of two paintings executed after his 1906 visit, Simpson wrote, "Am anxious that you should go Southwest again and am disposed to help so far as our rather small advertising fund will permit." Back again, Leigh "was actually immersed in the chasm, surrounded by its pinnacled glory. In this baptismal font the gloomy picture of Santa Fe's advertising budget faded away into unimportance . . . "[84] In 1909, he wrote in his journal: "Though I am perched far out on this naked tongue of rock where any wandering current of air would surely find me, though I huddle as closely under my sketching umbrella as I can, yet the perspiration trickles from my elbow. And this, let me add, means something in this dry atmosphere. . . . Some of my colors are melting and only by judicious tilting of the palette are prevented from sliding off."[85]

Of all the places he painted, Gunnar M. Widforss (1879–1934) "came to love the Grand Canyon best. He spent most of the latter part of his life along the rim, painting its various moods from sunrise to sunset."[86] He also painted on the canyon floor. "One of Widforss's obsessions in his Canyon work was to depict the enormous depths. Certain of his pictures do this with great force."[87] "With his easel and paint box he was a familiar silhouette along the Canyon rim drives and trails. He looked the part of a well-dressed surveyor or engineer in a heavy shirt, knee breeches, high laced boots, sweater and cap. He always wore a necktie. . . ."[88] After Widforss's death at the Grand Canyon, a 7,800-foot-high peak on its northern rim was named Widforss Point.

Painting For Love, Not Money

Simpson bargained shrewdly in negotiating the price of paintings. He once wrote to Couse, "Am wondering if you have any Indian subject, extra large size, which would fit into that space [the new ticket office in Los Angeles], and if so about what the cost would be. To be perfectly frank, we cannot afford to pay museum prices, but it just occurred to me that you might happen to have something on hand on the bargain counter, so to speak, which we could afford to purchase, on a reasonable installment plan."[89]

Simpson preferred to "pay" for paintings in railroad transportation and lodging. One Taos artist, Oscar E. Berninghaus (1874–1952) wrote to Simpson in 1914, "In answer to your question of what my price would be, I might say that I am planning a trip through the Southwest for this summer especially along your lines with the idea of remaining some 2 or 3 months. In figuring out what my transportation would cost me, I find that it will run in the neighborhood of 125.00. I am sure you will agree with me that this would be a low price for the painting, and will accept this either in cash—mileage or some other form of transportation—whatever is agreeable to you."[90] In 1915, he wrote to Simpson again, to tell him that he was submitting a painting of the Grand Canyon, ". . . believing it will be of interest and for the purpose of sale—I am asking

125.00—the greater part of which I will use for transportation for myself and family to Santa Fe and return. It is my hope to again make the annual South-west visit and shall feel encouraged if my proposition is favorable to you."[91]

When Simpson did pay for paintings, it was often on the installment plan, and then not promptly. Ernest

Blumenschein wrote to Simpson in 1911: "Am terribly disappointed that I can't have the money at once. I'll have to borrow somewhere, as I figure my resources up to the last notch, counting on you as the last notch."[92] Another time, he wrote, "The terms you mention are all agreeable, although I would rather have seen something coming along in advance. For ease of mind, I mean."[93] Artists also offered to complete paintings in different sizes for different prices. Writing to Simpson about *Evening at the Taos Pueblo,* (later renamed *Evening at Pueblo at Taos*) Blumenschein offered it on either a 25" x 30" canvas for $600, or a 34" x 40" at $800.[94]

Simpson Passes On

In 1933, after a long and successful career, William Simpson died. Tributes and memorials abounded. "Three loves dominated Mr. Simpson's life," eulogized *The Santa Fe Magazine.* "One was for his family; one for his railroad; one for that vast, indefinable, question-stirring workshop of God that those of us who live in it think of unconsciously as the Santa Fe Southwest."[95] "He died as he had always hoped to do, in the harness, still a potent factor in the strength and greatness he had done so much to build. It would have broken his heart to be retired." During his life, Simpson had been regarded affectionately by his colleagues for "the sudden light of his twisted smile, the twinkle that often crept into his eyes, his certain, quiet courtesy and dry wit. . . . He was a poet at heart, as well as a practical executive. He loved good pictures and good books, and thought deeply on his own account. . . . Among all Southwestern communities, Mr. Simpson loved best Old Santa Fe, New Mexico. To his memory the *Santa Fe New Mexican* offered this full tribute:

For half a century the late William Haskell Simpson, veteran official of the Santa Fe Railway Company . . .

devoted himself untiringly to the building up of New Mexico and all that vast empire known as the Santa Fe Southwest.

As general advertising manager for the railway company for a generation, he was closely identified with the promotion of New Mexico's development in its every phase. It would be quite impossible to estimate how much New Mexico owes him for its progress during that period.

. . . [H]e was in charge of what has been for all these years probably the most elaborate, ambitious and effective program of development-publicity ever inaugurated by any railroad. The Santa Fe Company has led the field in . . . selling Santa Fe service, and the . . . southwest territory, its resources and opportunities, to the world.

Mr. Simpson was a slight, shrewd, humorous, modest and delightful personality. . . . No veteran of the railway was more beloved. His heart was deeply in his work and in the Southwest. Especially did he love New Mexico and Santa Fe. . . .

His feeling for this old, sunny Spanish and Indian land, its tradition, its pueblos and placitas, and its soul, was very deep and understanding.[96]

A few years before his death, Simpson published a book of his poetry, *Along Old Trails: Poems of New Mexico and Arizona*. One poem in particular described his philosophy of life and death and was a poignant reminder of the beloved man:

Remembered Faces

Those left behind
Weep, For one who goes away
Alone —
Their hands reach out. . . .

Strange!
That I, going away,
Do not weep;
That I smile
At the remembered faces.

　　—William H. Simpson[97]

Simpson's dream lived on. Through the years, his successors have continued to build the art collection, and its parent company exhibits the collection throughout the country; it serves as an eloquent good-will ambassador and touchstone for the memories and marvels that are the "Santa Fe Southwest."

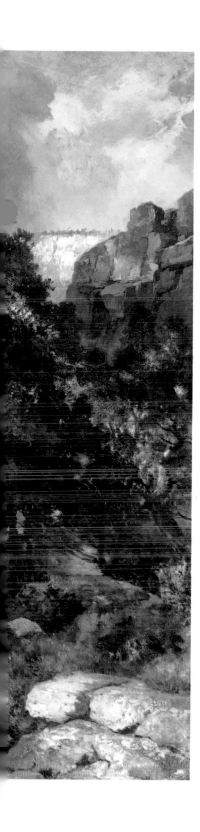

Sir Thomas Moran (1837–1926)

Grand Canyon, oil on canvas, 30"×40", acquired 1912.
"An inferno, swathed in soft celestial fires; a whole
chaotic under-world, just emptied of primeval floods
and waiting for a new creative word; a boding,
terrible thing, unflinchingly real, yet spectral as a
dream, eluding all sense of perspective or dimension,
outstretching the faculty of measurement, overlapping
the confines of definite apprehension. . . . A labyrinth
of huge architectural forms, endlessly varied in design,
fretted with ornamental devices, festooned with lace-
like webs formed of talus from the upper cliffs and
painted with every color known to the palette in pure
transparent tones of marvelous delicacy. Never was
picture more harmonious, never flower more exquis-
itely beautiful. It flashes instant communication of all
that architecture and painting and music for a
thousand years have gropingly striven to express. It is
the soul of Michael Angelo and of Beethoven." (C. A.
Higgins, *Grand Cañon of the Colorado River, Arizona*
[Chicago: Passenger Department Santa Fe Route,
1893], 10.)

Louis Akin (1868–1913)

El Tovar Hotel, Grand Canyon, oil on canvas, 25"×50",
acquired 1907. "The most unique, most comfortable,
and one of the costliest resort hotels in the Southwest
has recently been built by the Santa Fe at the railway
terminus and not far from the head of Bright Angel
Trail. It is named El Tovar, after Don Pedro de
Tovar, a Spanish conquistador whose name is linked
with the discovery of the Grand Canyon by
Coronado's men in 1540." (W. J. Black, *Hotel El
Tovar: The Grand Canyon of Arizona* [Chicago: Fred
Harvey, 1909], 2.)

Bertha Menzler Dressler (1871–1947)

San Francisco Peaks, oil on canvas, 30"×40", acquired 1903. "Simpson arrived in August and spent a full day touring around the San Francisco Peaks . . . and before leaving Flagstaff Simpson expressed his views: 'The San Francisco Peaks are the one great attraction and do more to advertise Flagstaff to travelers than any other thing, because they stand out for themselves." —W. H. Simpson (Bruce B. Babbitt, *Color and Light: The Southwestern Canvases of Louis Akin* [Flagstaff: Northland Press, 1973], 61.)

Charles Craig (1846–1931)

Indians Attacking Overland Train, oil on canvas, 24"×36", acquired 1907. "Pretty soon one of the gang would do something to make the Indians angry and then they would come. And if one of our men would happen to kill an Indian, the Indians always made it a point to get a white man in return. It didn't make any difference whether he was the guilty man or not, any white man would do. But most of the time we got along pretty well with the Indians."—"Red" MacKay, one of the builders of the Santa Fe line. (Ernest W. Hall, "The Red Captain of the Santa Fe," *The Santa Fe Magazine* 7 [February 1921], 27–8.]

Alonzo "Lon" Megargee (1891–1960)

Old Santa Fe Trail, oil on canvas, 24"×32", acquired 1912. "His restless independence as a man and an artist was clear then and remained so until his death. Always one characteristic stood out. He was indigenous. He belonged here. Not a carpet-bagger with a paint box, or a disillusioned urbanite seeking a new life, but an artist who used what he knew and had lived to put down what he had seen." —Scottsdale artist Lew Davis (*Arizona Living* [10 January 1975].)

William Herbert "Buck" Dunton (1878–1936)
The Old Santa Fe Trail, oil on canvas, 26"×32", acquired
1923. "The west has passed—more's the pity. In
another twenty-five years the old-time westerner will
have gone too—gone with the buffalo and the
antelope. I'm going to hand down to posterity a bit of
unadulterated *real thing* if it's the last thing I do—and
I'm going to do it *muy pronto.*"—Buck Dunton (Laura
M. Bickerstaff, *Pioneer Artists of Taos* [Denver: Sage
Books, 1955; reprint edition Denver: Old West
Publishing Co., 1983], 34.)

Frank Paul Sauerwein (1871–1910)

First Santa Fe Train Crossing Plains, oil on canvas, 30"×50", acquired 1907. "Every transcontinental or important railroad in America follows an Indian trail: and the Indian trail followed a deer trail or buffalo trail: and the common object of the buffalo, the Indian and the railroad is to 'get there,'... It was an accident that the Santa Fe route when it followed the line of least resistance across 'the Great American Desert' skimmed the cream of the artist's interest of the Southwest. There is no railroad in the world . . . which penetrates such a wonderland of the pictorial in geography and in humanity." (Charles F. Lummis, "The Artists' Paradise," *Out West* 29 [September 1908], 191.)

Charles Henry Harmon (1859–1936)

Indian Pueblo—Acoma, oil on canvas, 30"×40", acquired 1907. "There is one Acoma. It is a class by itself. The peer of it is not in the world. . . . It is a labyrinth of wonders of which no person alive knows all. . . . The longest visit never wears out its glamour; one feels as in a strange, sweet, unearthly dream—as among scenes and beings more than human, whose very rocks are genii, and whose people swart conjurors. It is spendthrift of beauty." (Charles F. Lummis, *The Land of Poco Tiempo* [New York: Charles Scribner's Sons, 1893], 41.)

Louis Akin (1868–1913)

The Temple, Grand Canyon, oil on canvas, 24"×24", acquired 1912. "The Grand Canyon is not a solitude. It is a living, moving, pulsating being, ever changing in form and color, pinnacles and towers springing into being out of unseen depths. From dark shades of brown and black, scarlet flames suddenly flash out and then die away into stretches of orange and purple. How can such a shifting, animated glory be called 'a thing?' It is a being, and among its upper battlements, its temples, . . . its cathedral spires, its arches and its domes, and in the deeper recesses of its inner gorge its spirit, its soul, the very spirit of the living God himself lives and moves and has its being." —R. B. Stanton (*Grand Canyon of Arizona* [Chicago: Passenger Department of the Santa Fe, 1909], 49.)

Elbridge Ayer Burbank (1858–1949)

Hastin-Gaha-Bitzi and *Ta-Jolle-Bijuie,* both oil
on canvas, each 30"×17", acquired 1910. "Burbank
journeyed to Gallup, New Mexico in search of the
Navajo. . . . 'Among the Navajos there is a curious
division of property,' Burbank wrote . . . , 'The hogan,
the sheep, and the goats belong to the women. The
horse saddles and jewelry belong to the men. . . . The
Navajo family ties are close. They are particularly
devoted to their children, who learn to ride ponies
before they can walk, so that they can follow the
flocks along with their elders. The children help their
parents in herding sheep, and sometimes they do all
the work themselves. They are good herders.' " (*The
End of the Trail,* Anshutz Corporation.)

Alice Cleaver (1878–1944)

Pueblo Home Scene, oil on canvas, 34"×46", acquired
1907. "Glance inside the houses! The upstairs portion
is evidently the living-room, for the fireplace is here
and the pot is on. Off the living-room are corn and
meal bins; and you can see the *metate* or stone, on
which the corn is ground by the women as in the days
of the Old Testament." (Agnes C. Laut, "Taos, An
Ancient American Capital," *The Santa Fe Magazine 7*
[September 1913], 28.)

E. Irving Couse (1866–1936)

Taos Indian Shepherd, oil on canvas, 35"×46", acquired 1907. "Couse knew immediately on his arrival in Taos that he had found the ideal subject for painting—the light-skinned, poetic, peaceful Indian in a native, natural setting far more beautiful than he had . . . envisioned. . . . To this artist settings were almost as important as the figure and here, wherever he looked, was a perfect backdrop—river, lush valleys, pines, quaking aspen, soft-lined, soft-colored adobe houses, sunsets and sunrises of unequalled splendor. . . ." (Alta Edmondson, "E. Irving Couse, Painter of Indians," *Panhandle-Plains Historical Review* 42 [1969], 12.)

Ernest L. Blumenschein (1874–1960)
Evening at Pueblo at Taos, oil on canvas, 30"×40", acquired 1913. "My grunting horse carried me down and across the gorges, around the foothills, over long flat spaces that were like great lakes of sagebrush through twenty slow miles of thrilling sensation. It had to end in the Taos valley, green with trees and fields of alfalfa, populated by dark-skinned people who greeted me pleasantly. Then I saw my first Taos Indians, picturesque, colorful, dressed in blankets artistically draped. New Mexico had gripped me. . . ."
—Ernest L. Blumenschein (Laura M. Bickerstaff, *Pioneer Artists of Taos* [Denver: Sage Books, 1955; reprint ed. Denver: Old West Publishing Co., 1983], 17.)

E. Irving Couse (1866–1936)

Wal-si-see (*Good Medicine*), oil on canvas, 21"×24",
acquired 1912. "Only the drum is confident, it thinks
the world has not changed; the beating heart, the
simplest of rhythms. . . . only . . . the strong Tribal
drum, and the rockhead of Taos mountain, remember
that civilization is a transient sickness." — Robinson
Jeffers (Arrell Morgan Gibson, *The Santa Fe and Taos
Colonies: Age of the Muses, 1900–1942* [Norman: University of Oklahoma Press, 1983], 179.)

E. Irving Couse (1866–1936)
The Hopi Kachina, oil on canvas, 24"×29", acquired
1929. "The Hopi Indians believe that the Kachina is a
super-natural being who is impersonated by a man
wearing a mask. The Kachinas are similar to Christian
saints and are supposed to carry prayers to the Hopi
gods that live on the San Francisco Peaks of Arizona
and other high mountains. . . . The dolls are hand-
carved from dry cottonwood roots and painted in
bright colors. There are about 200 different classifica-
tions of Kachina dolls and for many years they have
been treasured items of Indian lore." (Legend on back
of Fred Harvey menu, n.d. [Santa Fe: The Rainbow
Man Collection].)

E. Irving Couse (1866–1936)

The Pueblo Weaver, oil on canvas, 24"×30", acquired 1916. "Their contribution to art has been invaluable. We come out here to learn from them and find an apparently inexhaustible store of beauty and original-ity. I have seen Indian rugs whose beauty of design, texture and color were as fine as any Persian rug that has been woven. They are absolutely different in character, of course, but quite as valuable from artistic standpoint." (Ernest L. Blumenschein and Bert G. Phillips, "Appreciation of Indian Art," *El Palacio* 6 [24 May 1919], 179.)

E. Irving Couse (1866–1936)

Turquoise Bead Maker, oil on canvas, 24"×29", acquired 1925. "Turquoise is a native product, highly prized by the Indians. It is mainly used for necklaces, finger rings and bracelets. Necklace beads are patiently drilled by hand. The drill consists of an upright piece with a socket at the lower end which contains a sharp pointed iron drill. A cross-bar with strings is attached to the top of the upright. By working this cross-bar up and down with the right hand a rotary motion of great velocity is produced. Its piercing quality is greatly enhanced by the addition of a heavy disk just above the drill." (Unpublished essay by E. Irving Couse, n.d. [Chicago: Santa Fe Railway Archives].)

Oscar E. Berninghaus (1874–1952)

Pueblo of Taos, oil on canvas, 41"×81", acquired 1914.
"And so the artists came to Taos and to Santa Fe to
live and to paint the beauty they found there . . . the
Indian living much as he had for centuries caring for
the fragile land and living in his communal houses. . . .
Those who came to Santa Fe and Taos wanted to hold
their discovered places intact to retain a purity they
had sensed when they found it. They wished to keep
'progress' at bay, but they knew that this was impossible." (James T. Forrest, "The American Landscape
and the West," *Standing Rainbows: Railroad Promotion of
Art, the West and Its Native People.* A Special Exhibition
of Paintings from the Collection of the Atchison,
Topeka & Santa Fe Railway [Topeka: Kansas State
Historical Society, May 3–June 4, 1981].)

60

Oscar E. Berninghaus (1874–1952)

A Showery Day, Grand Canyon, oil on canvas, 30"×40", acquired 1915. "Nor elsewhere . . . may you look from any vantage-point upon such square leagues of inverted and captive skies—of rainbows in solution, and snow-storms, and thunder-storms far below you, and brimming fogs that flow with the moon, and with dawn ebb and ebb—till one by one the wide, voiceless tide reveals the glorious 'islands' of glowing peaks." (Charles F. Lummis, *Mesa, Cañon and Pueblo* [New York: The Century Company, 1925], 29.)

William Robinson Leigh (1866–1955)
Grand Canyon, oil on canvas, 36"×60", acquired 1911.
"I saw . . . the Grand Canyon. I knew that some of the
most distinctive, characteristic, dramatic, poetic,
unique motifs in the world were here in this virgin
country waiting an adequate hand to do them justice."
—William R. Leigh (Raymond Carlson, *Gallery of
Western Paintings* [New York: McGraw Hill Book
Company, 1951], 25.)

William Robinson Leigh (1866–1955)

Grand Canyon, oil on canvas, 28"×34", acquired 1913.
"The rock . . . I am tempted to believe, has a more
fiery hue than usual, as if it were glowing red hot. I
think an egg would fry beautifully on it. . . . The fierce
light dazzles. Oh! for a breeze. There is a torpor . . . a
spell upon the atmosphere. . . . Suddenly the peak I
have been painting is plunged in shadow. . . . A low
rumble explains the reason. Above Point Yuma the
vanguards of a storm are hurrying up the sky. . . . And
now the spell is broken. . . . The black giant is
growling and grumbling. . . . I gather up my belong-
ings and retire to the shelter of an overhanging ledge
of rocks where, after anchoring everything . . . I
stretch myself upon the ground and scornfully bid the
giant do his worst." —William R. Leigh (June
DuBois, *W. R. Leigh: The Definitive Illustrated Biography*
[Kansas City: The Lowell Press, 1977], 60–62.)

Elliott Daingerfield (1859–1932)

The Lifting Veil, Grand Canyon, oil on canvas, 32"×48", acquired 1913. "One is amazed to perceive that the canvas follows not a literal transcript of any scene but a marvelous recreation of the glowing color and wild grandeur of the place. The entire painting sings out with gorgeous color—opal mountains and crimson peaks are touched with mists of pearl and pink, and the chasms between them vibrate with many colored shadows. . . . Daingerfield spreads the paint on the canvas in broad masses and leaves the texture of the pigment rather rough in order to break up the surface. The roughness of one layer of paint constitutes a surface on which successive layers of color are superimposed in much the same way as the teeth of a comb catch strands of hair. The effect of one through another, the increased luster of tone upon tone, and the magic carrying power of certain colors for certain others hints at innumerable shades of feeling that one could not have conceived with a more direct approach." (Robert Hobbs, *Elliott Daingerfield Retrospective Exhibition* [Charlotte, North Carolina: The Mint Museum of Art, 1971], 47–48.)

Edward Henry Potthast (1857–1927)

Bright Angel Canyon, Grand Canyon, oil on canvas, 31"×41", acquired 1911. "Once an artist who loved the wilderness brought his bride to the head of the Bright Angel Trail. . . . [S]he looked out across the miles and miles of tumult of form and riot of color that seemed to swirl thousands of feet below her and around her. As from the clouds she looked down into an illimitable, red-tinged, ash-colored hell, abandoned and turned to stone aeons and aeons ago, she stared amazed at the awful thing for a long minute, and then, as the tears of inexplicable emotion dimmed her eyes, she turned and cried vehemently at her artist husband: 'If you ever try to paint that, I'll leave you!'"
—William Allen White (*The Grand Canyon of Arizona: Being A Book of Words from Many Pens, About the Grand Canyon of the Colorado River in Arizona* [Chicago: Santa Fe Railway, 1909], 63.)

Joseph Jacinto "Jo" Mora (1876–1947)

Hopi Women Preparing for Harvest Dance, watercolor, 10"×9", acquired 1916; *Hopi Indian Maiden,* watercolor, 20"×14", acquired ca. 1907. "I am back at Tolchaco for a couple of weeks in which time I am going to make a tour of this part of the reservation to sketch and photograph. After that I'm going to saddle up once more and cross the Painted Desert for the third time into Hopi Land. This time I will go straight to Walpi where I expect to stay about a month, painting and sketching and living with E. A. Burbank, the well-known Indian painter. I met him at Oraibi and he seems to have taken quite a liking to me, for he insists on my going to Walpi and then going around with him to other Indian tribes. During my stay of four days at Walpi, I got in some good licks, making several pen and inks and two water colors, one of a Hopi maiden with her hair done up in the proper Hopi style for maidens." —Jo Mora (Tyrone H. Stewart, "Jo Morra [sic] Photographs 1904–1907," *Southwest Art* 6 [Winter 1977–78], 35–36.)

69

70

Louis Akin (1868–1913)

Street Scene, Hopi Pueblo, oil on canvas, 29"×21", acquired 1907. "The town is arranged in irregular rows of terraced houses, rising, as a rule, to the height of three stories. . . . The writer must confess that when he trod these streets for the first time six years ago, the sensation was not only indescribable, but utterly unlike that produced by a visit to any other Indian town either before or since." (George A. Dorsey, *Indians of the Southwest* [Chicago: Passenger Department, Atchison Topeka & Santa Fe Railway System, 1903], 111–12.)

72

Marion Kavanaugh Wachtel (1873–1954)
Pueblo of Walpi, watercolor, 24"×32", acquired 1929;
Evening, Pueblo of Walpi, watercolor, 18"×21", acquired
1910. "Pass on through the streets of Walpi with its
terraced house row on one side and the precipice on
the other, pass through the arch, on out to the point of
the mesa—what a panorama is spread out at one's
feet!" (George A. Dorsey, *Indians of the Southwest*
[Chicago: Passenger Department, Atchison Topeka &
Santa Fe Railway System, 1903], 109.)

Louis Hovey Sharp (1875–1946)

Buffalo Dance at Mishongnovi, oil on canvas, 26"×37",
acquired 1913. "Then suddenly they came. Out of the
wide, white universe, out of myth and legend, out of
the depths of America itself. They came filing into the
open plaza, shaking their gourd rattles, uttering their
strange cries. A line of figures part man, part beast,
part bird. Bare bodies splotched with paint, sinuously
bending at the waist. . . . They began dancing. . . . No
longer man nor beast nor bird, but embodied forces of
earth and sky swirling across the sea of snow from the
blue mountains on the horizon. . . . Dancing as gods
have always danced before their people." (Frank
Waters, _Masked Gods_ [Athens: Swallow Press, 1950;
reprint ed., 1989], 12.)

Alonzo "Lon" Megargee (1891–1960)

Indian Dance, oil on canvas, 30"×40", acquired 1925. "I heard the singing and drumming as soon as we reached the Pueblo, and it drew me strongly and I left the others and ran hurriedly towards it with my heart beating. . . . a volume of sound . . . was the glad, solemn voice of the tribe, and at the same time it was like the wind that rose and fell above us. . . . I heard the voice of the One coming from the Many. . . . " (Mabel Dodge Luhan, *Edge of Taos Desert: An Escape to Reality* [New York: Harcourt, Brace and Company, 1937], 62–63.)

Grace Ravlin (1873–1956)

San Geronimo Day, Taos, oil on canvas, 26"×32",
acquired 1917. "Well Friday, I went off . . . to see the
Indian dance. It was blistering hot down there. . . .
We crawled up a ladder on top of one of the flat
adobe Indian houses and we almost drew a bigger
crowd than the dance. . . . There were a good many
artists there, but I was the only one that painted. I
could only make notes but still it was a beginning and
some day I'll have these dances nailed down."
—Grace Ravlin (Ravlin to Alta R. Turner, 17 July
1916 [New York: Alta Ann Morris Papers].)

Bert Geer Phillips (1868–1956)

The Secret Olla, oil on canvas, 25"×29", acquired 1918.
" 'The Indians worship all things beautiful,' Phillips
said. Theirs was not the passive appreciation characteristic of other cultures; rather, the Indians' response
to beauty was an integral part of their being. Their
religion, Phillips perceived, revolved around the
rhythm and life of nature. Their love of beauty was
born of knowledge as well as of what we call supersti-
tion." (Laura M. Bickerstaff, *Pioneer Artists of Taos*
[Denver: Sage Books, 1955; reprint ed. Denver: Old
West Publishing Co., 1983], 57.)

Bert Geer Phillips (1868–1956)
Indian Girl, oil on canvas, 12"×9", acquired 1907; *Taos Indian,* oil on canvas, 18"×14", acquired 1907. "Sometimes I ask myself why I remain away from the 'Land of Civilization' but never before have I tried to formulate a reply. I have simply been content to stay on. The charm of the great stretches of mountain and plains and the interest of their inhabitants is never ending. As I visit their villages and talk with my Indian friends, I see and hear the young bucks wrapped in their white blankets standing on the bridge singing a love song in the moonlight, and I feel the romance of youth, so the answer comes as I write and I believe that it is the romance of this great pure-aired land that makes the most lasting impression on my mind and heart." —Bert Geer Phillips (Patricia Janis Broder, *Taos: A Painter's Dream* [Boston: New York Graphic Society, 1980], 97.)

Carl Oscar Borg (1879–1946)

Sunset Canyon de Chelly, oil on canvas, 30"×40",
acquired 1916. ". . . Borg's and O'Keeffe's vision of
the Southwestern landscape show striking similarities.
O'Keeffe's elimination of the superficial while still
maintaining the integrity of the subject results in some
of the greatest achievements in American painting.
Many of her paintings of single hills or cliffs have
assumed iconic proportions. Carl Oscar Borg's *Sunset
Canyon de Chelly* . . . achieves this same emblematic
appeal. . . . this painting is a celebration of the color,
light, and form unique to the landscape of the
American Southwest. . . . It may be Borg's master-
piece." —Michael R. Grauer, Curator of Art, Panhandle-Plains Historical Museum, Canyon, Texas
(Katherine Plake Hough, Michael R. Grauer, Helen
Laird, *Carl Oscar Borg: A Niche in Time* [Palm Springs:
Palm Springs Desert Museum, n.d.].)

Gerald Cassidy (1879–1934)

Canyon de Chelly, oil on canvas, 32"×26", acquired 1945.

"This valley is not ours, nor these mountains,
Nor the names we give them—they belong,
They, and this sweep of sun washed air,
Desert and hill and crumbling earth,
To those who have lain here long years
and felt the soak of the sun
Through the red sand and crumbling rock,
till even their bones were part of the
sun-steeped valley."
—Alice Corbin Henderson (Arrell Morgan Gibson,
The Santa Fe and Taos Colonies: Age of the Muses, 1900–1942 [Norman: University of Oklahoma Press, 1983], 267.)

Jessie Benton Evans (1866–1954)

Spring on the Desert, oil on canvas, 36"×40", acquired 1930. "The desert, exotic, terrible, fabulous—what is it, and where? While the reality is no myth, its fangs have been drawn. . . . Seen through the double window of a Pullman, the desert is a progressive experience. Yet not an impressive one, particularly . . . The landscape is arid, there is a conspicuous lack of running streams, the hills are thinly spotted with dwarf cedars. . . . Such is the indefinite margin of the Land of Little Rain." (Ross Calvin, *Sky Determines: An Interpretation of the Southwest* [Albuquerque: The University of New Mexico Press, 1948], 35.)

Marjorie Helen Thomas (1885–1983)
Navajo Indians at Desert Water Hole, oil on canvas,
20"×30", acquired 1910. "Then, too, in much of our
western landscape we need the Indian in the same
way that a finely wrought piece of gold needs a jewel
to set off its beauty in a piece of jewelry." (*The Art of
Oscar Berninghaus* [Chicago: Young's Art Galleries,
1919], 3.)

Alonzo "Lon" Megargee (1891–1960)
Camelback Mountain, oil on canvas, 26"×36", acquired 1953. "If you have a chord for the heroic, hardly shall you find another land so invigorating as this of Arizona. It stiffens the mental fiber like a whiff of the north wind. It stirs in the blood dim echoes of days when achievement lay in the might of the individual arm. . . . The super-refinement of cities dissipates here. There is a tonic breeze that blows toward simple relations and a lusty self-hood." —C. A. Higgins (Katherine L. Chase, "Brushstrokes on the Plateau," _Plateau_ [January 1984], 12.)

87

Gerard C. Delano (1890–1972)

Navajo Ponies, oil on canvas, 30"×36", acquired 1942.
"There is a vastness, an immensity, and a peaceful
hush of an enormous cathedral about Arizona's great
canyons. Whoever has been within these walls, and
has seen the flocks of sheep and goats grazing, heard
the distant tinkle of the lead goat's bell, listened to the
haunting song of the bright-skirted shepherdess, and
who has seen in the distance an approaching rider — a
tiny speck against the massive canyon walls — must
yearn to perpetuate his impressions of those precious
moments. That is why I paint the canyon and the
Navajo. The Navajo people are a proud and beautiful
race of great dignity. It is my idea to show them as I
know them. . . . " — Gerard C. Delano (Richard G.
Bowman, "Gerard Curtis Delano," *Artists of the Rockies
and the Golden West* [Spring 1980], 36.)

Bettina Steinke (b. 1913)

Navajo Woman at Ganado, oil on canvas, 20"×24",
acquired 1956. "Southwestern Indians have no better
friends than artists, who recognize that the Indian is
essentially an artist. They value his art in all its forms,
they help him without condescension, and they
respect his integrity too much to try to make him over
into something foreign." (Erna Fergusson, *Dancing
Gods* [New York: Alfred A. Knopf, 1942], v.)

Gerald Cassidy (1879–1934)

Temple of Nar-Sus-Sa, oil on canvas, 30"×40", acquired 1945. "The distinctive character of the Southwest's vast emptiness, massive mountains, deep canyons, vari-colored arroyos, rugged mesas and desert flats captured the artist-visitor's eye. The special quality of light in this part of the country provided artists with a fresh challenge in the handling of light and form. . . . Such environmental phenomena as brilliantly colored skies, mountains bleached by intense sunlight, and swiftly traveling thunderhead clouds casting sharp shadows across mesas were impressive to behold. Horizontal spaces, extreme coloration and dramatic geological features demanded that artists find new formal solutions and varied approaches to painting the desert landscape." (Katherine Plake Hough, Michael R. Grauer, Helen Laird, *Carl Oscar Borg: A Niche in Time* [Palm Springs: Palm Springs Desert Museum, n.d.].)

E. Martin Hennings (1886–1956)
Navajo Silversmith, oil on canvas, 25"×30", acquired
1956; *Navajo Sandpainter,* oil on canvas, 26"×30"
acquired 1956. "It was quite an experience working
on the Navajo Reservation. . . . I was fortunate
enough to meet a nurse from the Presbyterian
hospital. . . . She knew the Indians for miles around
and spoke the Navajo language. With her assistance I
was able to select models and make arrangements for
posing which I did at their homes. . . . John Nez who
posed for the silversmith is only a part time worker in
silver. James Smith who posed for 'The Sand Painter'
is a true Medicine Man, and the only one of my sitters
who could talk English." — E. Martin Hennings
(Hennings to Arthur Dailey [Chicago: Santa Fe
Archives, 27 January 1956].)

Charles Waldo Love (1881–1967)

Monument Valley, oil on canvas, 30"×40", acquired 1946. "Doubtless the hardest thing of all to paint is that glorious stuff which we cannot see, but which makes everything beautiful that we do see; which is too thin for our eyes to grasp, and yet so potent that without it they would pop out of their sockets; which is tasteless, yet without which we could never take another bite; which is colorless, yet tinges everything on earth—the Air. The atmosphere of the Southwest is perhaps the hardest in the world for artists to catch. It is so subtle, so magical, so mixed with witchcraft, that it fools the sharpest eye and laughs at the cleverest palette. . . . An air that brings the very rocks to life, that glows and broods upon the desert until strange unrealities fill the world and one sits in the beautiful presence of a dream. . . . " (Charles F. Lummis, "The Artist's Paradise," *Out West* 29, [September 1908], 191.)

94

Harry Paul Burlin (1886–1969)

The Navajo, oil on canvas, 36"×28", acquired 1916.
"Burlin's sketches of the Navajos (a people still as
richly suggestive to the painter as any in the world)
strike deeply and instantly far below the surface to the
essential mood-values, as it were, of the life of a
nomad shepherd folk adrift on the Arizona Desert."
—Natalie Curtis, Burlin's ethnomusicologist wife
(Natalie Curtis, "A New Art in the West," *The
International Studio* 63 [November 1917], xvii.)

LaVerne Nelson Black (1887–1938)

Along the Old Trail, oil on canvas, 30"×40", acquired 1927. " . . . for a *greatness* of beauty I have never experienced anything like New Mexico . . . with the sage-brush desert sweeping grey-blue in between, dotted with tiny cube-crystals of houses, the vast amphitheatre of lofty, indomitable desert, sweeping round to the ponderous Sangre de Cristo mountains on the east, and coming up flush at the pine-dotted foot-hills of the Rockies! What splendour! Only the tawny eagle could really sail out into the splendour of it all. . . . " —D. H. Lawrence (Keith Sagar, ed., *D. H. Lawrence and New Mexico* [Salt Lake City: Gibbs M. Smith, Inc., 1982], 17.)

LaVerne Nelson Black (1887–1938)

Apache Hunting Party, oil on canvas, 20"×30", acquired
1929. "Some of the most notable tribes of . . . no-
mads—like the Navajos, whose blankets and silver
work are pre-eminent, and the Apaches, who, man
for man have been probably the most successful warriors in history—all these, and a great deal more,
make the Southwest a wonderland without a parallel."
—Charles F. Lummis (*The Grand Canyon of Arizona*
[Chicago: Passenger Department of the Santa Fe,
1909], 35.)

LaVerne Nelson Black (1887–1938)

Going to the Pueblo, oil on canvas, 32"×40", acquired 1931. "We finally came along close to the mountain. It swept away above us, and there at the foot of it was the Pueblo. . . . On either side of a sparkling brown stream that rushed down from a canyon. . . . two big community houses were standing in a smooth, clear space of earth, absolutely stark and undecorated. . . . Now, strange to say, although the village seemed austere and certainly anything but domestic, yet one got a feeling of home from it. The very essence of it was of the home. Why? I do not know. That was the feeling it gave out richly. A stab of longing and of nostalgia went through me like lightning." (Mabel Dodge Luhan, *Edge of Taos Desert: An Escape to Reality* [New York: Harcourt, Brace and Company, 1937], 56–57.)

Ila McAfee (b. 1898)

Taos Pueblo Summer Afternoon, oil on canvas, 30"×36", acquired 1930. "[Taos] was so different then, the village was small and the Indians remained uninfluenced by the invaders. Once I asked one of them, 'What did you call this country before the Europeans came?' 'Ours,' he told me." —Ila McAfee (Rita Simmons, "Ila McAfee," *Southwest Art* [September 1990], 100.)

Ernest L. Blumenschein (1874–1960)

Taos Indian Holding Water Jug, oil on canvas, 30"×25", acquired 1911. "The art of the Indians is not only beautiful, but it is unique. Originality is a priceless donation to all human endeavor and the aboriginal American has actually contributed more to the arts than two hundred years of 'civilized' occupation of North America has produced." (Ernest L. Blumenschein and Bert G. Phillips, "Appreciation of Indian Art," *El Palacio* 6 [24 May 1919], 179.)

Walter Ufer (1876–1936)

Taos Girls, oil on canvas, 30"×30", acquired 1916. "A vast old religion which once swayed the earth lingers in unbroken practice there in New Mexico. . . . You can feel it, the atmosphere of it, around the pueblos. . . . go to Taos pueblo on some brilliant snowy morning and see the white figure on the roof: or come riding through at dusk on some windy evening, when the black skirts of the silent women blow around the white wide boots, and you will feel the old, old roots of human consciousness still reaching down to depths we know nothing of. . . ." —D. H. Lawrence (Keith Sagar, ed., _D. H. Lawrence and New Mexico_ [Salt Lake City: Gibbs M. Smith, Inc., 1982], 96–97.)

Victor Higgins (1884–1949)
Three Women of Taos, oil on canvas, 35"×40", acquired
1916. "A painter paints a canvas not because he wants
to make a 'picture' as that he wants to solve a problem. A problem in form, in construction, design if you
prefer the term, in color harmonies. . . . " —Victor
Higgins (Ina Sizer Cassidy, "Art and Artists of New
Mexico," *New Mexico Magazine* [December 1932], 22.)

E. Martin Hennings (1886–1956)
Contemplation, oil on canvas, 14"×16", acquired 1954.
"... A painting is a great adventure — thinking over a subject, making all sorts of pencil sketches, designing, comparing, organizing, planning its color, the lighting, until you are sure it has everything that you want [in order to be] strong and effective. Then you go to work on your canvas, with your models, and this will call for all the ability and craftsmanship which the years of work have given you, plus all the special effort you are capable of in order to have a consummative and significant piece of art realized." — E. Martin Hennings (Robert R. White, *The Lithographs and Etchings of E. Martin Hennings* [Santa Fe: Museum of New Mexico Press, 1978].)

105

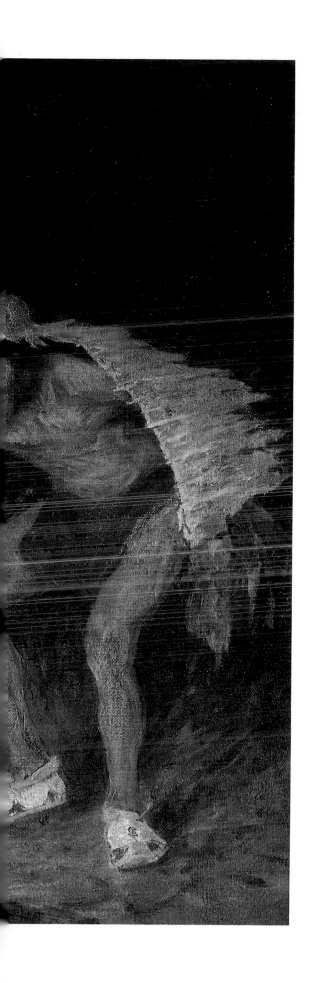

E. Irving Couse (1866–1936)

The Eagle Dance, oil on canvas, 24"×29", acquired 1921.
"This South-west, which is but one chapter of our rich
tradition, is our own authentic wonderland—a
treasure-trove of romantic myth—profoundly
significant and beautiful, guarded by ancient races
practicing their ancient rites, in a region of incredible
color and startling natural grandeur." —Harriet
Monroe (Marta Weigle and Kyle Fiore, *Santa Fe and
Taos: The Writer's Era, 1916–1941* [Santa Fe: Ancient
City Press, 1982], 17.)

E. Irving Couse (1866–1936)

The Flute Dance, oil on canvas, 24"×29", acquired 1922.
"The cacique or medicine-man knows the mythology
which lies behind the ceremonies and he understands
the significance of the various forms, but his knowledge is sacred to him and he will not divulge it lightly.
. . . 'Unless we do it this way, our prayer will not be
answered. This is the way of the ancients.' " (Erna
Fergusson, *Dancing Gods* [New York: Alfred A.
Knopf, 1942], xv.)

Bert Geer Phillips (1868–1956)
Taos Indian, oil on canvas, 19"×15", acquired 1907.
"I see, far in the west . . . a limitless ravine,
with plains and mountains dark,
I see swarms of stalwart chieftains,
medicine-men, and warriors,
As flitting by like clouds of ghosts, they pass and
are gone in the twilight . . ."
(Walt Whitman, *Leaves of Grass* [New York: The
Heritage Press, n.d.], 459.)

Joseph H. Sharp (1859–1953)
Old War Bonnet, oil on convas, 26"×29", acquired 1916.
"Mr. Sharp . . . is a typical American, full of tact,
energy and ingenuity. He is intensely human and has
always treated the Indian as a brother . . . . He peeps
into their hearts. His vivid imagination sees things
from their viewpoint. He feels the thrill of things that
thrill his subjects and so he puts the living spirit, not
merely the technically exact portrait, upon his
canvas." (Laura A. Davies, "An Indian Painter of the
West," *El Palacio* 13 [1 September 1922], 66.)

Warren E. Rollins (1861–1962)

A Song in the Kiva, oil on canvas, 26"×20", date of acquisition unknown. "The Indians keep burning an eternal fire, the sacred fire of the old dark religion. To the vast white America, either in our generation or in the time of our children or grandchildren, will come some fearful convulsion. Some terrible convulsion will take place among the millions of this country, sooner or later. When the pueblos are gone. But oh, let us have the grace and dignity to shelter these ancient centres of life, so that, if die they must, they die a natural death. And at the same time, let us try to adjust ourselves again to the Indian outlook, to take up an old dark thread from their vision, and see again as they see, without forgetting we are ourselves" —D. H. Lawrence (Keith Sagar, ed., _D.H. Lawrence and New Mexico_ [Salt Lake City: Gibbs M. Smith, Inc., 1982], 17.)

Ferdinand Burgdorff (1858–1949)

Interior Isleta Mission, oil on canvas, 24"×30", acquired 1917. "The big clumsy doors of the church were open, and presently some of the newcomers entered with their basket offerings, crossing themselves at the door, and disposed their baskets, their candles, and their knees at certain points along the rude floor of loose boards laid flat on smooth adobe. It was not at random that they took these scattered positions. These were they whose relatives had enjoyed the felicity of being buried under the church floor; and each knelt over the indistinguishable resting-place of her loved and lost. . . . The altar flared with innumerable candles which twinkled on ancient saints, . . . on mirrors and tinsel and paper flowers. Through the three square, high, dirty windows in the five-foot adobe wall the sunlight strained, lighting up vaguely. . . the kneeling figures . . . ." (Charles F. Lummis, *A Tramp Across the Continent* [New York: Charles Scribner's Sons, 1893], 150.)

Warren E. Rollins (1861–1962)

Indian Water Carrier, oil on canvas, 31"×38", acquired 1913. ". . . I tried to . . . remain in the other world I had left behind me, in that Pueblo where the women sat quietly in full, starched calico dresses, or silently walked down to the river with shawls over them, to fetch water which they carried home in round, clay pots balanced upon their heads, one arm stretched up with the long shawl-line falling straight down in lovely folds." (Mabel Dodge Luhan, *Edge of Taos Desert: An Escape to Reality* [New York: Harcourt, Brace and Company, 1937], 179.)

Warren E. Rollins (1861–1962)

Street Scene Oraibi, oil on canvas, 24"×36", acquired
1915. "Again descending into the plain and crossing
the valley, we ascend by a comparatively easy trail to
that oldest and largest Hopi pueblo, Oraibi. Oraibi
numbers nearly one thousand inhabitants, and as
Taos is to-day the easternmost of all pueblos, so, in
Oraibi, we have come to the western limit of the living
pueblos. Oraibi occupies to-day the same spot where
in 1540 Coronado, the first of the Conquistadores,
penetrated this hitherto unknown world. . . ." (George
A. Dorsey, *Indians of the Southwest* [Chicago: Passenger
Department, Atchison Topeka & Santa Fe Railway
System, 1903], 110.)

Benjamin Blessum (1877–unknown)
Indian Pueblo of Santa Clara, oil on canvas, 25"×29",
acquired 1916. "Marsden Hartley, who painted in the
Taos area in 1918 and 1919, wrote perceptively of the
intensity of light he experienced there. New Mexico
was not, he said, 'a country of light on things' but was
rather 'a country of things in light.' " (Kay Aiken
Reeve, "Santa Fe and Taos, 1898–1942: An American
Cultural Center," *Southwestern Studies* Monograph 67
[El Paso: Texas Western Press, 1965], 5.)

Gerald Cassidy (1879–1934)

The Priestesses, oil on canvas, 40"×30", acquired 1933. "Any man who is really an artist will find the Southwest the most imminent and audible prompting of God that he has ever encountered. No other cue is so like to make him forget his audience and only remember his past, as a region where the ingenuity, the imagination, and the love of God are so visible at every turn. . . . It is high time for the artists to come upon the Southwest." (Charles F. Lummis, "The Artist's Paradise," *Out West* 29 [September 1908], 181.)

Gunnar Widforss (1879–1934)

Phantom Ranch, Grand Canyon, watercolor, 24"×21", acquired 1925. "David Rust set up a permanent hunting camp at the bottom of the Grand Canyon in 1903—calling it 'Rust Camp.' Four years later Rust built a tramway sixty feet above the Colorado River and for the first time visitors could make their way over the river in a cage attached to a cable. Theodore Roosevelt visited the camp in 1913, afterward, the name was changed to 'Roosevelt's Camp.' In 1932 Mary Jane Colter designed and Fred Harvey Co. completed construction of Phantom Ranch on the site of 'Rust Ragtache/Roosevelt Camp' to accommodate riders on their mule trips into the Canyon." (Unpublished "History," [Chicago: Santa Fe Railway, 1990], 6.)

118

Gunnar Widforss (1879–1934)

Grand Canyon, watercolor, 24"×33", acquired 1933. "I have seldom seen anything as bewitching as the purple and rose flames that glow in the canyon depths of those Western paintings. For the ecstatic joy of vivid yet elusive color, give me almost any one of the Grand Canyon pictures. Here the design is of tremendous importance. But, like the structure of that marvel of nature, it is not obvious. You see the shelving rocks, the vast chasms . . . and you feel the abyss that yawns below the plane of your vision. . . . To get those flame-and-mist tones Mr. Widforss must have dipped his brush in magic." —Emily Grant Hutchings, art critic (Bill and Frances Spencer Belknap, *Gunnar Widforss, Painter of the Grand Canyon* [Flagstaff: Northland Press, for the Museum of Northern Arizona, 1969], 75–82.)

Carl Oscar Borg (1879–1946)

Hermit Camp, Grand Canyon, oil on canvas, 30"×40", acquired 1917. "He met and became friends with another Swedish-American, Charles A. Brant, the manager of the El Tovar Hotel who gave him room and board in exchange for a promised Canyon picture. In December . . . Borg sent a completed Canyon painting to Brant [who] wrote to thank him. 'Now my dear friend, I know I told you that you possessed extraordinary gifts as an artist. . . . I am not coming to this conclusion from my own observation, but we have here with us today the dean of America's landscape painters, Mr. Thomas Moran, and Mr. Moran stated to me in the hearing of a dozen others that he considered you preeminently the highest grade of any artist in America today. Mr. Moran is not a man who slops over in praise of other artists' work —in fact, quite the reverse. Mr. Moran stated that we did not have a painting of the Canyon in the hotel today that comes anywhere near showing the artistic skill displayed in the picture you sent me.' " (Katherine Plake Hough, Michael R. Grauer, Helen Laird, *Carl Oscar Borg: A Niche in Time* [Palm Springs: Palm Springs Desert Museum, n.d.].)

O. B. Jacobson (1882–1966)
Grand Canyon, oil on canvas, 42"×32", acquired 1916.
"Some five hundred Jacobson canvases, in public and
private collections around the world, portray the
artist's self-stated devotion to 'interpret the grandeur
of the Southwest' in the vivid simplicity of his . . .
style. Sweeping lines, uncluttered surfaces, powerful
brush strokes and rich colors characterize . . . his
paintings." (Reference Report, Western History
Collections, Library, The University of Oklahoma
[1973].)

Walter Ufer (1876–1936)

Grand Canyon from El Tovar, oil on canvas, 24"×30", acquired 1915. "The Hotel El Tovar stands near the rim of the Canyon with a level stretch of a hundred feet lying between it and the very edge. A low parapet marks the edge and a number of benches are ranged along for the silent contemplation of the view. Beyond the wall there is nothing. It is as though the wall marked the end of the world and the beginning of infinity." (John T. McCutcheon, *Doing the Grand Canyon* [Chicago: Fred Harvey, 1909], 5.)

William Penhallow Henderson (1877–1943)
The Pink Adobe, oil on canvas, 18"×24", acquired 1918;
Midsummer in New Mexico, oil on canvas, 18"×24",
acquired 1918. "We wound our way up the canyon.
Sometimes it was narrow and the dark green trees
climbed above us on both sides; and sometimes it
widened out into valleys where fruit orchards lay
dreaming. At several places Mexican adobe houses
nestled cozily under great cottonwood trees beside the
river." (Mabel Dodge Luhan, *Edge of Taos Desert: An
Escape to Reality* [New York: Harcourt, Brace and
Company, 1937], 33.)

Sheldon Parsons (1866–1943)

October in New Mexico, oil on canvas, 30"×40", acquired 1930. "My father [Sheldon Parsons] was the second painter to make Santa Fe his home, and he was the first to become director of Fine Arts of the Museum of New Mexico. . . . But soon after our arrival in 1913 many more and many famous painters came to Santa Fe, some to take up residence but most of them to come only for a summer or so, or for occasional visits." —Sara Parsons Mack (Edna Robertson and Sarah Nestor, *Artists of the Canyons and Caminos* [Salt Lake City: Gibbs M. Smith, Inc., 1982], 29.)

Edgar Spier Cameron (1862–1944)

The Land of Poco Tiempo, oil on canvas, 24"×32", acquired 1940. "Sun, silence, and adobe—that is New Mexico in three words. . . . It is the Great American Mystery—the National Rip Van Winkle—the United States which is *not* the United States. Here is the land of *poco tiempo*—the home of 'Pretty Soon.' Why hurry with the hurrying world? The 'Pretty Soon' of New Spain is better than the 'Now! Now!' of the haggard States. The opiate sun soothes to rest, the adobe is made to lean against, the hush of day-long noon would not be broken. Let us not hasten—*mañana* will do. Better still, *pasado mañana.*" (Charles F. Lummis, *The Land Of Poco Tiempo* [New York: Charles Scribner's Sons, 1893], 1.)

Theodore Van Soelen (1890–1964)

Tesuque Valley, oil on canvas, 34"×36", acquired 1925.
"When oldtimers grumbled about the arrival of new
settlers and wanted to rid the town of them, Soely
proclaimed, 'Give me variety or give me a pass on the
Santa Fe.' . . . he didn't think that 'painters should
swim in schools like fish.' " (Marian F. Love, "A
Distinguished Painter: Theodore Van Soelen," *The
Santa Fean* [January–February 1980], 40.)

Theodore Van Soelen (1890–1964)

Acequia Madre (*Deep Shadows*), oil on canvas, 42"×48",
acquired 1928. "Many pictures have come out of
the Santa Fe region of New Mexico in recent years,
says Henry McBride in the *Sun*, but few have had
the 'allure' of those of Theodore Van Soelen, who
'. . . actually "sells" the place to us,' remarked Mr.
McBride. 'If reproductions of the pictures were used
on the railway time-tables, the trains to Santa Fe,
Taos, etc., would be far more crowded than they are
at present . . . he has a very nice feeling about Santa
Fe and makes it plain to the bystanders.' " ("New
York Criticism," *The Art Digest* [1 January 1936], 18.)

William Herbert "Buck" Dunton (1878–1936)
Trail in the Foothills, oil on canvas, 20"×16", acquired
1917. "When I was a little boy and lived in Maine I
read everything about the West I could get my hands
on—not dime novels, but everything authentic. I lived
the life in prospect. Then I lived it in actuality, living
with cowpunchers in Montana, Nevada, Wyoming,
New Mexico, Arizona—all along the cattle strip. Now
that those days are gone, I live it in retrospect and in
my pictures." —Buck Dunton (Patricia Janis Broder,
Taos: A Painter's Dream [Boston: New York Graphic
Society, 1980], 173.)

E. Martin Hennings (1886–1956)

Canyon Aspens, oil on canvas, 30"×30", acquired 1925.
"In the fall of the year when he went to the Hondo
Canyon every day to paint the golden aspen, occa-
sionally my mother would pack a picnic lunch and go
along with him. While he painted she'd read or hunt
for wildflowers to bring back for the garden. . . . He
was a wonderful father, never too busy to put down
his brushes and palette to listen to my problems when
I interrupted him in his studio. His family and his
work were his whole life and he succeeded in making
the most of all his God-given gifts." —Helen
Hennings Winton (Unpublished essay, n.d., Museum
of Fine Arts, Museum of New Mexico Archives.)

133

Walter Ufer (1876–1936)

The Desert Trail, oil on canvas, 20"×25", acquired 1926. "I paint the Indian as he is. In the garden digging—In the field working—Riding amongst the sage— Meeting his woman in the desert—Angling for trout—In meditation." —Walter Ufer (*Walter Ufer 1876–1936: Sixteen Paintings* [Houston: Christie, Manson and Woods Int'l. Inc., 1982].)

135

E. Martin Hennings (1886–1956)
Edge of the Sage, oil on canvas, 30"×30", acquired 1936.
"Landscape plays so important a part in my work, and
subjects of sage, mountain and sky. Nothing thrills me
more, when in the fall, the aspens and cottonwoods
are in color and with the sunlight playing across
them—all the poetry and drama, all the moods and
changes of nature are there to inspire one great
accomplishment from year to year." —E. Martin
Hennings (Robert R. White, *The Lithographs and
Etchings of E. Martin Hennings* [Santa Fe: Museum of
New Mexico Press, 1978].)

NOTES

1. Keith Sagar, ed., *D. H. Lawrence and New Mexico* (Salt Lake City: Gibbs M. Smith, Inc., 1982), 43.

2. *The Grand Canyon of Arizona: Being a Book of Words From Many Pens, About the Grand Canyon of the Colorado River In Arizona* (Chicago: Passenger Department of the Santa Fe, 1909), 87.

3. Charles F. Lummis, quoted in an article by George Wharton James, *Overland Monthly*, May 1923.

4. *The Grand Canyon of Arizona*, 33.

5. Sagar, *D. H. Lawrence and New Mexico*, 17.

6. Kay A. Reeve, "Pueblos, Poets and Painters: The Role of the Pueblo Indians in the Development of the Santa Fe-Taos Region as an American Cultural Center," *American Indian Culture and Research Journal* 5 (1981): 16.

7. Ellis T. Clarke, "Alien Element in American Art," *Brush and Pencil*, 7 (October 1900).

8. *New York World*, 1 February 1920.

9. "Fifty Years of Santa Fe History," *The Santa Fe Magazine* 17 (January 1923), 28.

10. Ree Sheck, ed., *Railroads and Railroad Towns in New Mexico* (Santa Fe: New Mexico Magazine, 1989), 3.

11. Charles F. Lummis, *The Land of Poco Tiempo* (New York: Charles Scribner's Sons, 1893), 181–182.

12. "Fifty Years of Santa Fe History," *The Santa Fe Magazine* 17 (January 1923), 35.

13. Ibid., 44.

14. Ibid., 36.

15. Ibid., 40.

16. Ibid., 43.

17. Edward Hungerford, "A Study in Consistent Railroad Advertising," *The Santa Fe Magazine* 19 (March 1923): 44.

18. Ibid., 45.

19. Ted Schwarz, "The Santa Fe Railway and Early Southwest Artists," *American West* (October 1982), 32. 83

20. Timothy Manns, *A Guide to Grand Canyon Village* (Grand Canyon: Grand Canyon National History Association), 1.

21. "The Harvey System," *The Santa Fe Magazine* 1 (July 1907): 271–72.

22. Keith L. Bryant, Jr., *History of the Atchison, Topeka & Santa Fe Railway* (New York: Macmillan, 1974; reprint ed., Lincoln: University of Nebraska Press, 1974), 107.

23. Lesley Poling-Kempes, *The Harvey Girls: Women Who Opened the West* (New York: Paragon House, 1989), 31.

24. "How Fame Has Been Won for the Harvey Service by Devotion to a Business Principle," *The Santa Fe Magazine* 10 (February 1916): 35.

25. "Fred Harvey Coat Rule Upheld by Oklahoma Supreme Court," *The Santa Fe Magazine* 18 (November 1924): 29.

26. Bryant, *The Atchison, Topeka & Santa Fe Railway*, 111.

27. "How Fame Has Been Won for the Harvey Service," 31.

28. Bryant, *The Atchison, Topeka & Santa Fe Railway*, 114.

29. Toby Smith, "Those Harvey Girls," *Impact Magazine, Albuquerque Journal* (11 August 1981): 9.

30. Ibid., 8.

31. S. J. Allen, *Fred Harvey Meals* (Chicago: Poole Brothers, 7 July 1909).

32. Sylvanus Griswold Morley, "Development of the Santa Fe Style of Architecture," *The Santa Fe Magazine* 9 (June 1915): 25.

33. Marta Weigle, "From Desert to Disneyworld: The Santa Fe Railway and the Fred Harvey Company Display the Indian Southwest," *Journal of Anthropology Research* 4561 (Spring 1989): 115–133.

34. *Las Vegas Hot Springs and Surroundings Near Las Vegas, New Mexico: The Karlsbad of America* (Chicago: Passenger Department Santa Fe Route, 1887), 14.

35. Ibid., 39.

36. Bryant, *The Atchison, Topeka & Santa Fe Railway*, 111.

37. W. J. Black, *Hotel El Tovar: The Grand Canyon of Arizona* (Chicago: Fred Harvey, 1909), 1.

38. Ibid., 2.

39. Charles F. Lummis, "The Artist's Paradise," *Out West* 29 (September 1908): 181.

40. Hungerford, "Consistent Railroad Advertising," 45.

41. Keith L. Bryant, Jr., "The Origins and Development of the Santa Fe Railway Collection of Western Art," *Standing Rainbows: Railroad Promotion of Art, the West and Its Native People*. A Special Exhibition of Paintings from the Collection of the Atchison, Topeka & Santa Fe Railway. (Topeka: Kansas State Historical Society, 3 May 1981–4 June 1981).

42. *Chicago Times Herald*, 6 December 1896.

43. Alfred Runte, *Trains of Discovery—Western Railroads and the National Parks* (Flagstaff: Northland Press, 1985), 12.

44. Hungerford, "Consistent Railroad Advertising," 46.

45. Ibid., 48.

46. Bruce B. Babbitt, *Color and Light: The Southwestern Canvases of Louis Akin* (Flagstaff: Northland Press, 1973), xi.

47. Ibid., 9.

48. Ibid., 21.

49. Elaine Haher Harrison, "Frank Paul Sauerwein," *Panhandle-Plains Historical Review* 33 (1960): 28.

50. Ibid., 29.

51. Charles F. Lummis, *Mesas and Canyons* (New York: Charles Scribner's Sons, 1925), 10.

52. Ibid., 504.

53. Laura M. Bickerstaff, *Pioneer Artists of Taos* (Denver: Sage Books, 1955; reprint ed. Denver: Old West Publishing Company, 1983), 16.

54. Patricia Trenton and Patrick T. Houlihan, *Native Americans, Five Centuries of Changing Images* (New York: Harry N. Abrams, Inc., 1989), 81.

55. Virginia Couse Leavitt, "E. Irving Couse," *Southwest Profile*, (March/April 1986), 15.

56. Alta Edmondson, "E. Irving Couse, Painter of Indians." *Panhandle-Plains Historical Review* 42 (1969): 12.

57. Couse to Simpson (Chicago: Santa Fe Railway Archives), 20 February 1925.

58. Simpson to Couse (Chicago: Santa Fe Railway Archives), 17 March 1951.

59. Simpson to Couse (Tucson: Couse Family Archives), 10 October 1934.

60. T. C. McLuhan, *Dream Tracks: The Railroad and the American Indian* 1890–1930 (New York: Harry N. Abrams, Inc., 1985), 19.

61. Robert A. Trennert, "Fairs, Expositions, and the Changing Image of Southwestern Indians, 1876–1904." *New Mexico Historical Review* 62 (April 1987): 128.

62. Helen Hennings Winton essay (Santa Fe: Museum of Fine Arts Archives).

63. Van Deren Coke, *Taos and Santa Fe: The Artist's Environment, 1882–1942* (Albuquerque: University of New Mexico Press for the Amon Carter Museum of Western Art, 1963), 24.

64. Trenton and Houlihan, *Native Americans*, 63.

65. Ibid., 101.

66. James Taylor Forrest, *William Penhallow Henderson Retrospective Exhibition, July 21–August 20, 1963* (Santa Fe: Museum of Fine Arts, Museum of New Mexico, 1963), 6.

67. Frank Waters, *Masked Gods* (Athens: Swallow Press, 1950; reprinted., 1989), 109.

68. John Wiley, "Dropping in on Fred Harvey from the Caon to Chicago," *The Santa Fe Magazine* 23 (January 1929): 44–46.

69. Virginia L. Grattan, *Builder Upon the Red Earth* (Flagstaff: Northland Press, 1980), 10–13.

70. McLuhan, *Dream Tracks*, 45.

71. Gretchen Faulkner, *Forgotten Connections: Maine's Role in the Navajo Textile Trade* (Orono, Maine: Lecture, Hudson Museum, 1990).

72. Waters, *Masked Gods*, 111.

73. Grattan, *Builder Upon the Red Earth*, 19.

74. Ibid., 2.

75. *Indian-Detours Roundabout Old Santa Fe New Mexico* (Chicago: A.T. & S.F.R.R., 1908).

76. Beatrice Chauvenet, *A Courier on the Indian Detour of the Santa Fe RR.* (Santa Fe: Unpublished Manuscript, January 1991).

77. Simpson to Moran, (Chicago: Santa Fe Railway Archives), 29 April 1908.

78. W. Thetford LeViness, "The Altar of the Gods," *The Kansas City Star*, (6 August 1961).

79. Arlene Jacobowitz, *Edward Henry Potthast, 1857 to 1927* (New York: The Chapellier Galleries, 1969).

80. Katherine L. Chase, "Brushstrokes on the Plateau," *Plateau* 56 (January 1984): 11.

81. Arlene Jacobowitz, *Edward Henry Potthast, 1857 to 1927* (New York: The Chapellier Galleries, 1969).

82. Robert Hobbs, *Elliot Daingerfield Retrospective Exhibition* (Charlotte, N.C.: Mint Museum of Art, 1971), 48.

83. Chase, "Brushstrokes on the Plateau," 14.

84. June DuBois, *W. R. Leigh: The Definitive Illustrated Biography* (Kansas City: The Lowell Press, 1977), 57.

85. Ibid., 60.

86. Bill Belknap and Frances Spencer, *Gunnar Widforss, Painter of the Grand Canyon* (Flagstaff: Museum of Northern Arizona, 1969), 38.

87. Ibid., 40.

88. Ibid., 51.

89. Simpson to Couse, 27 July 1926 (Chicago: Santa Fe Railway Archives).

90. Berninghaus to Simpson, 25 March 1914 (Chicago: Santa Fe Railway Archives).

91. Berninghaus to Simpson, 29 March 1915 (Chicago: Santa Fe Railway Archives).

92. Blumenschein to Simpson, 19 September 1911 (Chicago: Santa Fe Railway Archives).

93. Blumenschein to Simpson, 11 June 1911 (Chicago: Santa Fe Railway Archives).

94. Blumenschein to Simpson, 26 March 1913 (Chicago: Santa Fe Railway Archives).

95. "William H. Simpson Passes On," *The Santa Fe Magazine* (June 1933): 43–44.

96. Ibid., 44.

97. William Haskell Simpson, *Along Old Trails: Poems of New Mexico and Arizona* (Boston and New York: Houghton Mifflin Company 1929), 80.

BIBLIOGRAPHY

Books

Allen, S. J. *Fred Harvey Meals.* Chicago: Poole Brothers, 7 July 1901.

Babbitt, Bruce B. *Color and Light: The Southwestern Canvases of Louis Akin.* Flagstaff: Northland Press, 1973.

Belknap, Bill and Frances Spencer. *Gunnar Widforss, Painter of the Grand Canyon.* Flagstaff: Museum of Northern Arizona, 1969.

Berkhofer, Robert F. *The White Man's Indian: Images of the American Indian from Columbus to the Present.* New York: Alfred A. Knopf, 1978.

Bickerstaff, Laura M. *Pioneer Artists of Taos.* Denver: Sage Books, 1955; reprint ed. Denver: Old West Publishing Co., 1983.

Bowman, Richard G. *Walking With Beauty: The Art and Life of Gerard Curtis Delano.* Boulder: Richard G. Bowman, 1990.

Broder, Patricia Janis. *Taos: A Painter's Dream.* Boston: New York Graphic Society, 1980.

_____. *The American West: The Modern Vision.* Boston: Little Brown & Co., 1984.

Brody, J.J. *Indian Painters & White Patrons.* Albuquerque: University of New Mexico Press, 1971.

Bryant, Keith L., Jr. *History of the Atchison, Topeka & Santa Fe Railway.* New York: Macmillan, 1974; reprint ed., Lincoln: University of Nebraska Press, 1974.

Bynner, Witter. *Indian Earth.* New York: Alfred A. Knopf, 1929.

Burbank, Elbridge A. and Ernest Royce. *Burbank Among the Indians.* Caldwell, ID: Caxton Printers Ltd., 1944.

Calvin, Ross. *Sky Determines: An Interpretation of the Southwest.* Albuquerque: The University of New Mexico Press, 1964, 1948.

Coke, Van Deren. *Taos and Santa Fe: The Artist's Environment, 1882–1942.* Albuquerque: University of New Mexico Press for the Amon Carter Museum of Western Art, 1963.

D'Emilio, Sandra and Suzan Campbell. *Spirit and Vision: Images of Ranchos de Taos.* Santa Fe: Museum of New Mexico Press, 1977.

Dorsey, George A. *Indians of the Southwest.* Passenger Department, Atchison Topeka & Santa Fe Railway System, 1903.

Dowdy, Doris Ostrander. *Artists of the American West: A Biographical Dictionary.* 3 vols. Chicago: The Swallow Press, Inc., 1974–1985. Athens: Ohio University Press.

Dubois, June. *W. R. Leigh: The Definitive Illustrated Biography.* Kansas City: The Lowell Press, 1977.

El Tovar, Grand Canyon of Arizona. New York, Chicago: Norman Pierce Company.

Fergusson, Erna. *Our Southwest.* New York: Alfred A. Knopf, 1940.

_____. *Dancing Gods.* New York: Alfred A. Knopf, 1942.

Gibson, Arrell Morgan. *The Santa Fe and Taos Colonies: Age of the Muses, 1900–1942.* Norman: University of Oklahoma Press, 1983.

Goetzmann, William H. and William N. Goetzmann. *The West of the Imagination.* New York and London: W. W. Norton & Company, 1986.

The Grand Canyon of Arizona: Being a Book of Words From Many Pens, About the Grand Canyon of the Colorado River in Arizona. Chicago: Passenger Department of the Santa Fe, 1909.

Grattan, Virginia L. *Builder Upon the Red Earth.* Flagstaff: Northland Press, 1980.

Harmsen, Dorothy. *Harmsen's Western Americana.* Flagstaff: Northland Press, 1971.

Harvey, Fred. *The Great Southwest: Along the Santa Fe.* Kansas City, MO: Fred Harvey, 1914.

Higgins, C. A. *Grand Canon of the Colorado River, Arizona.* Chicago: Passenger Department of the Santa Fe Route, 1893.

_____. *Titan of Chasms: The Grand Canyon of Arizona.* Chicago: Passenger Department of the Santa Fe Route, 1905.

Indian-Detours Roundabout Old Santa Fe New Mexico. Chicago: A. T. & S. F. R. R. Company, 1908.

Laird, Helen. *Carl Oscar Borg and the Magic Region.* Layton, Utah: Peregrine Smith Books, 1986.

Las Vegas Hot Springs and Surroundings Near Las Vegas, New Mexico: The Karlsbad of America. Chicago: Passenger Department Santa Fe Route, 1887.

Luhan, Mabel Dodge. *Intimate Memories.* Vol. 3. *On the Edge of Taos Desert: An Escape to Reality.* New York: Harcourt, Brace, 1937.

_____. *Taos and Its Artists.* New York: Duell, Sloan and Pearce, 1947.

Lummis, Charles F. *The Land of Poco Tiempo.* New York: Charles Scribner's Sons, 1893.

_____. *Mesa, Cañon and Pueblo.* New York: Century Company, 1925.

Manns, Timothy. *A Guide to Grand Canyon Village.* Grand Canyon: Grand Canyon National History Association, n.d.

Marx, Leo. *The Machine in the Garden.* New York: Oxford University Press, 1964.

Marshall, James. *Santa Fe: The Railroad that Built an Empire.*

New York: Random House, 1945.

McLuhan, T.C. *Dream Tracks: The Railroad and the American Indian 1890–1930*. New York: Harry N. Abrams, Inc., 1985.

McCracken, Harold. *Portrait of the Old West*. New York, Toronto, London: McGraw Hill Book Company, Inc., 1952.

McCutcheon, John T. *Doing the Grand Canyon*. D. Appleton & Co., 1909; reprint ed., Chicago: Fred Harvey, 1922.

Mead, Tray C., ed. *Capturing the Canyon*. Mesa, AZ: Mesa Southwest Museum, 1987.

Miller, Perry. *Errand into the Wilderness*. New York: Harper and Row, 1964.

Morrill, Claire. *A Taos Mosaic: Portrait of a New Mexico Village*. Albuquerque: University of New Mexico Press, 1973.

Poling-Kempes, Lesley. *The Harvey Girls: Women Who Opened the West*. New York: Paragon House, 1989.

Pomeroy, Earl. *In Search of the Golden West: The Tourist in Western America*. New York: Alfred A. Knopf, 1957.

Porter, Dean A. *Victor Higgins*. South Bend: Art Gallery of the University of Notre Dame, 1975.

Reeve, Kay Aiken. *Santa Fe and Taos, 1898–1942: An American Cultural Center*. Southwestern Studies Monograph 67. El Paso: Texas Western Press, 1982.

Robertson, Edna and Sarah Nestor. *Artists of the Canyons and Caminos: Santa Fe, the Early Years*. Salt Lake City: Gibbs M. Smith, Inc., 1982.

Runte, Alfred. *Trains of Discovery—Western Railroads and the National Parks*. Flagstaff: Northland Press, 1985.

Sagar, Keith, ed. *D.H. Lawrence and New Mexico*. Salt Lake City: Gibbs M. Smith, Inc., 1982.

Samuels, Peggy and Harold. *The Illustrated Biographical Encyclopedia of Artists of the American West*. New York: Double Day and Co., Inc., 1976.

Santa Fe de-Luxe. Chicago: Poole Bros., 1915.

Sheck, Ree, ed. *Railroads and Railroad Towns in New Mexico*. Santa Fe: New Mexico Magazine, 1989.

Schimmel, Julie. *The Art and Life of W. Herbert Dunton, 1878–1936*. Austin: The University of Texas Press, 1984.

Scully, Vincent. *Pueblo: Mountain, Village, Dance*. New York: The Viking Press, 1975.

Sherman, John. *Taos: A Pictorial History*. Santa Fe: William Gannon, 1990.

Simpson, William Haskell. *Along Old Trails*. Boston and New York: Houghton Mifflin Company, 1929.

Smith, Henry Nash. *Virgin Land: The American West as Symbol and Myth*. Cambridge: Harvard University Press, 1950, 1970.

Taft, Robert. *Artists and Illustrators of the Old West, 1850–1900*. New York: Charles Scribner and Sons, 1953.

Thomas, D. H. *The Southwestern Indian Detours*. Phoenix: Hunter Publishing Company, 1978.

Trenton, Patricia and Peter H. Hassrick. *The Rocky Mountains: A Vision for Artists of the Nineteenth Century*. Norman: University of Oklahoma Press, 1983.

Trenton, Patricia and Patrick T. Houlihan. *Native Americans, Five Centuries of Changing Images*. New York: Harry N. Abrams, Inc., 1989.

_____ and Patrick T. Houlihan. *Native Faces: Indian Cultures in American Art*. Los Angeles: Los Angeles Athletic Club and the Southwest Museum, 1984.

Udall, Sharyn Rohlfsen. *Modernist Painting in New Mexico 1913–1935*. Albuquerque: University of New Mexico Press, 1984.

Waters, Frank. *Masked Gods*. Athens: Swallow Press, 1950; reprint ed., 1989.

Weigle, Marta, and Kyle Fiore. *Santa Fe and Taos: The Writer's Era, 1916–1941*. Santa Fe: Ancient City Press, 1982.

Periodical Articles

Bell, Elizabeth E. "Old Santa Fe." *The Santa Fe Magazine* 26 (January 1932): 9–12.

Blumenschein, Ernest L. "Origin of the Taos Art Colony." *El Palacio* 20 (May 1926): 190–193.

Blumenschein, Ernest L. and Bert G. Phillips. "Appreciation of Indian Art," *El Palacio* 6 (24 May 1919): 178–179.

Bowman, Richard. "Gerard Curtis Delano—Master Painter of the Navajo." *Denver Westerners' Roundup* (May–June 1979): 5–23.

"Brushstrokes on the Plateau." *Plateau* 56 (January 1984): 2–32.

Bryant, Keith L., Jr. "The Atchison, Topeka and Santa Fe Railway and the Development of the Taos and Santa Fe Art Colonies." *Western Historical Quarterly* 9 (October 1978): 437–453.

D'Emilio, Sandra. "Touring Attractions." *Southwest Art* (May 1987):32–37.

Edmondson, Alta, "E. Irving Couse, Painter of Indians." *Panhandle-Plains Historical Review* 42 (1969): 1–22.

Fenn, Forrest. "Joseph Henry Sharp: The Taos Years." *New Mexico Magazine* (November 1983): 36–38.

"Fifty Years of Santa Fe History." *The Santa Fe Magazine* 17 (January 1923): 27–48.

"Fred Harvey Coat Rule Upheld by Oklahoma Supreme Court." *The Santa Fe Magazine* 18 (November 1924): 29–32.

Hall, Ernest W. "The Red Captain of the Santa Fe." *The Santa Fe Magazine* 12 (February 1921): 27–28.

Harrison, Elaine Haber. "Frank Paul Sauerwein." *Panhandle-Plains Historical Review* 33 (1960): 3–67.

Hartley, Marsden. "America as Landscape." *El Palacio* 5 (9 December 1918): 332–333.

_____. "Aesthetic Sincerity." *El Palacio* 5 (9 December 1918): 332–333.

"The Harvey Girls." *The Santa Fe Magazine* 40 (January 1946): 22–23.

"The Harvey System." *Santa Fe Employees' Magazine* 1 (July 1907): 271–277.

Henderson, James D. "Meals by Fred Harvey." *Arizona and the West*, 305–322.

"How Fame Has Been Won for the Harvey Service by Devotion to a Business Principle." *The Santa Fe Magazine* 10 (February 1916): 31–47.

Hungerford, Edward. "A Study in Consistent Railroad Advertising." *The Santa Fe Magazine* 19 (March 1923): 44–48.

Jensen, A. N. "The Academie Julian and the Academic Tradition in Taos." *El Palacio* 79 (December 1973): 37–42.

Leavitt, Virginia Couse. "E. Irving Couse." *Southwest Profile* (March–April 1986): 13–15.

Lieu, Jocelyn. "The Castaeda: New Owner Halts Decline of Opulent Hotel." *New Mexico Magazine* (February 1991): 70–73.

"Lon Megargee Show at Scottsdale." *Arizona Living* (10 January 1975): 12.

Lummis, Charles F. "The Artists' Paradise." *Out West* 28 (June 1908): 451; 29 (September 1908): 174–191.

Lynch, Dudley M. "Lamy: Railroad Junction." *New Mexico Magazine* (October 1966): 2–5.

Morley, Sylvanus Griswold. "Development of the Santa Fe Style of Architecture." *The Santa Fe Magazine* 9 (June 1915): 25–32.

"The New Alvarado Hotel at Albuquerque." *The Santa Fe Magazine* 16 (October 1922): 40–41.

Pettibone, W. H. "Reminiscent of Early Days On the Santa Fe." *Santa Fe Magazine* 8 (September 1914): 45–47.

Reeve, Kay A. "Pueblos, Poets and Painters: The Role of the Pueblo Indians in the Development of the Santa Fe–Taos Region as an American Cultural Center." *American Indian Culture and Research Journal* 5 (1981): 1–19.

_____. "The Making of An American Place." *New Mexico Quarterly* 21 (Spring 1951): 135–137.

Schwarz, Ted. "The Santa Fe Railway and Early Southwest Artists." *American West* (October 1982): 32–41.

Smith, Toby. "Homeward Bound." *Impact Magazine, Albuquerque Journal,* (3 February 1987).

_____. "Those Harvey Girls." *Impact Magazine, Albuquerque Journal,* (11 August 1981): 8–10.

Stewart, Tyronne H. "Jo Mora Photographs 1904–1907." *Southwest Art* 6 (Winter 1977–78): 31–38.

"Theodore Van Soelen, Santa Fe Artist." *El Palacio* 53 (January 1946): 1–3.

Trennert, Robert A. "Fairs, Expositions, and the Changing Image of Southwestern Indians, 1876–1904." *New Mexico Historical Review* 62 (April 1987): 127–151.

"The Waitresses Who Won the West." *The Albuquerque Tribune* (8 December 1989): Sec. D, 13.

Weigle, Marta. "Finding the 'True America'—Ethnic Tourism in New Mexico During the New Deal." *Folklife Annual '88–'89* (1989): 53–73.

_____. "From Desert to Disneyworld: The Santa Fe Railroad and the Fred Harvey Company Display the Indian Southwest." *Journal of Anthropology Research* (Spring 1989): 115–133.

Wiley, John. "Dropping in on Fred Harvey from the Cañon to Chicago." *The Santa Fe Magazine* 23 (January 1929): 43–48.

"William H. Simpson Passes On." *The Santa Fe Magazine* 44 (July 1933): 43–44.

Dissertations and Theses

Gaither, James M. "A Return to the Village: A Study of Santa Fe and Taos, New Mexico as Cultural Centers, 1900–1934." Ph.D. diss., University of Minnesota, 1957.

Henderson, James D. "Meals by Fred Harvey: A Phenomenon of the American West." Master's thesis, University of Arizona, 1965.

Plank, Arnold C. "Desert Versus Garden: The Role of Western Images in the Settlement of Kansas." Master's thesis, Kansas State University, 1962.

Reeve, Kay Aiken. "The Making of an American Place: The Development of Santa Fe and Taos, New Mexico, as an American Cultural Center, 1898–1942." Ph.D. diss., Texas A & M University, 1977.

Rushing, Jackson. "Native American Art and Culture and the New York Avant-Garde 1910–1950." Ph.D. diss., University of Texas, 1969.

Exhibition Catalogs

The Art of Oscar Berninghaus. Chicago: Young's Art Galleries, 1919.

Ballinger, James K. and Andrea D. Rubenstein. *Visitors to Arizona 1846–1980.* Phoenix: Phoenix Art Museum, 1980.

Carl Moon, Photographer and Illustrator of the American Southwest. San Francisco: Argonaut Book Shop, 1982.

Chase, Katherine L. *Brushstrokes on the Plateau: An Overview of Anglo Art on the Colorado Plateau.* Flagstaff: Museum of Northern Arizona Press, 1984.

Cunningham, Elizabeth, with George Schriever. *Masterpieces of the American West: Selections from the Anschutz Collection.* Denver: A. B. Hirschfeld Press for the Anschutz Collection, 1983.

D'Emilio, Sandra. E. Martin Hennings: *The Influence of New Mexico.* Santa Fe: Museum of New Mexico, 1987.

Eldredge, Charles C., Julie Schimmel, and William H. Truettner. *Art in New Mexico, 1900–1945: Paths to Taos and Santa Fe.* New York: Abbeville Press, for the National

Museum of American Art, Smithsonian Institution, Washington, D.C., 1986.

Gibson, Arrell M., *Santa Fe Collection of Southwestern Art: An Exhibition at Gilcrease Museum, Tulsa Oklahoma, 26 September–21 November 1983*. Foreword by Fred A. Meyers. Chicago: Santa Fe Railroad, 1983.

Hobbs, Robert. *Elliot Daingerfield Retrospective Exhibition*. Charlotte, N.C.: Mint Museum of Art, 1971.

Jacobowitz, Arlene. *Edward Henry Potthast, 1857 to 1927*. New York: The Chapellier Galleries, 1969.

Lucas, David J. *La Verne Nelson Black*. Phoenix: Valley National Bank, 1970.

A Retrospective Showing of Paintings by E. Irving Couse. Canyon, Texas: Panhandle Plains Historical Museum, 5–28 Feb. 1967.

Standing Rainbows: Railroad Promotion of Art, the West and Its Native People. A Special Exhibition of Paintings from the Collection of the Atchison, Topeka & Santa Fe Railway. Topeka: Kansas State Historical Society, 3 May 1981–4 June 1981.

Trenton, Pat. *Picturesque Images from Taos and Santa Fe*. Denver: Denver Art Museum, 1974.

Waloshuk, Nicholas, Jr. *Paintings by E. Irving Couse*. Palm Desert: Palm Desert Museum.

Walter Ufer 1876–1936: Sixteen Paintings. Houston: Christie, Manson and Woods Int'l. Inc..

Udall, Sharyn R. *Victor Higgins in New Mexico*. Corpus Christi: Art Museum of South Texas, 1984.

Unpublished Material

Chauvenet, Beatrice. *A Courier on the Indian Detour of the Santa Fe RR*. January 1990.

Couse, Virginia Leavitt. *Taos and the American Art Colony Movement: The Search for an American School of Art*. Unpublished manuscript, 1986.

Faulkner, Gretchen. *Forgotten Connections: Maine's Role in the Navajo Textile Trade*. Lecture, Hudson Museum, Orono, Maine, 1990.

INDEX